Angel Intelligence

© 2007 Kabbalah Centre International, Inc. All rights reserved.

No part of this publication may be reproduced or transmitted in any form or by any means, electronic or mechanical, including photocopying, recording, or by any information storage and retrieval system, without permission in writing from the publisher, except by a reviewer who wishes to quote brief passages in connection with a review written for inclusion in a magazine, newspaper, or broadcast.

Kabbalah Centre Publishing is a registered DBA of
Kabbalah Centre International, Inc.

For further information:

The Kabbalah Centre
155 E. 48th St., New York, NY 10017
1062 S. Robertson Blvd., Los Angeles, CA 90035

1.800.Kabbalah www.kabbalah.com

Printed in China, August 2025

ISBN: 978-1-952895-27-2
Angel Intelligence

Design: HL Design (Hyun Min Lee) www.hldesignco.com

Angel Intelligence

How Your Consciousness Determines Which Angels Come Into Your Life

From the Teachings of Rav and Karen Berg

Dear Sarah,

We dedicate this book to you!

May you always walk with grace and courage, with a heart full of love,
and a spirit that knows no boundaries.

May you find and fulfill your soul's purpose
and share this life's journey with your spiritual other.

May all those searching also be blessed to connect with their spiritual other.

May your days be filled with laughter, your nights with peace,
and your dreams with endless possibilities.

May you always be kind, not only to others… but to yourself as well.

As you grow, may you discover the strength within to face life's challenges
with resilience, and may your journey be illuminated by the Light of the Creator!

You are a precious gift, and we pray you know just how deeply you are cherished.

May the Creator open the hearts of all those who have a desire to connect
with the Angels!

We Love you infinitely,
Mom & Dad

TABLE OF CONTENTS

PREFACE xi

Part I: UNDERSTANDING OUR GLEAMING UNIVERSE

1. THE POWER OF ANGELS 3
2. THE INFRASTRUCTURE OF OUR UNIVERSE 5
3. BILLIONS OF ANGELS AT YOUR FINGERTIPS 7
4. ATOMIC ANGELS 10
5. CREATING ANGELS 13
6. THE POWER OF NEGATIVE AND POSITIVE ANGELS 15
7. WHY DO ANGELS EXIST, ANYWAY? 19
8. THE WIRING SYSTEM 22
9. WHY CAN'T WE SEE THEM? 25
10. WINDOWS AND BLINDS 26
11. TEENAGE WASTELAND 29
12. IT'S ALL IN YOUR HANDS 31
13. TOUCHED BY AN ANGEL 33
14. CREATING ANGELS: CHOOSING YOUR WORDS 36
15. CREATING ANGELS: CHOOSING YOUR ACTIONS 38
16. CREATING ANGELS: CHOOSING YOUR FRIENDS 40
17. CREATING ANGELS: USING YOUR POWER 42
18. FREE WILL AND DOUBT 43
19. DO ANGELS HAVE FREE WILL? 45

20. THE VEIL OF TIME 46
21. A FISH DOESN'T KNOW IT'S IN WATER 48
22. JACOB'S GLEAMING UNIVERSE 49

Part II: IT HELPS TO KNOW THE PLAYERS

23. ANGELS ON YOUR SHOULDER 54
24. MEET YOUR GUARDIAN ANGEL 57
25. NOW MEET YOUR OPPONENT 69
26. THE TEN SEFIROT: THE STRUCTURE OF 62
    THE UNIVERSE
27. THE ARCHANGELS 64
28. THE ARCHANGEL MICHAEL: CLOTHE YOURSELF 66
    IN MERCY
29. THE ARCHANGEL GABRIEL: THE PRINCE OF JUSTICE ... 68
30. THE ARCHANGEL URIEL: THE FIRE OF GOD 71
31. THE ARCHANGEL RAPHAEL: HEAL THE EARTH 72
32. RAZI"EL: THE PRIMORDIAL ANGEL 74
33. ANGELS OF THE DAY 76
34. THE ANGELS OF THE ZODIAC 79
35. ANGELS FOR OUR CHILDREN 83
36. THE ANGELS OF HAPPINESS 84
37. METATR"ON: FROM HUMAN TO ANGELIC 85
38. NEGATIVE ANGELS 86
39. A ROGUES' GALLERY 89
40. THE ANGELS OF DEATH 91
41. THE ANGELS OF THE CHAMBERS OF THE UNIVERSE ... 93
42. THE ANGELS OF JUDGMENT 95

Part III: SEND ME AN ANGEL

43. THE TECHNOLOGY OF THE SOUL 99
44. CONNECTING TO YOUR ANGELS 100
45. THE LETTERS OF THE ANGELS 105
46. HOW TO CONNECT TO THE VOICE OF YOUR 107
    GUARDIAN ANGEL
47. CALLING UPON THE ARCHANGELS 110
48. HOW TO CONTACT THE ANGELS OF THE DAY 111
49. HOW TO CONTACT THE ANGELS OF HAPPINESS 122
50. THE ANA BEKO'ACH: THE PRAYER OF 124
    THE KABBALIST

PREFACE

Have you ever suffered from loneliness? Had moments when you felt: "I'm struggling in this world all by myself?" It may be reassuring to know, then, that there are billions of angels to help guide you along your journey. There are some angels that will test you and some angels that you can call on to inspire you. In this book, you'll learn how angels work to shape your world—and how your actions actually have the power to create angels, for better or for worse. As you become aware of the angel intelligences at play in your life, this knowledge can give you strength and confidence as you face even the most fearsome challenges.

The majority of humankind—an estimated 98 percent of us—believe in angels. Odds are very good, therefore, that you're part of this group. But have you ever stopped to think about what you mean when you say you believe in angels? Are these the cute chubby cherubs that decorate 17th century Italian paintings? Or luminous winged beings in flowing white gowns awaiting your arrival at the pearly gates? Perhaps what comes to mind are actors you've seen in movies—say, a scruffy John Travolta as *Michael*, a wisecracking Will Smith in *The Legend of Bagger Vance*, or the more serious angel who visited stressed-out Jimmy Stewart in *It's a Wonderful Life*. Maybe you believe an angel is a departed loved one who looks out for you from his

or her lofty perch, keeping you on the straight and narrow, protecting you from harm.

Or perhaps they're just part of the randomness of the universe. You may not understand why angels seem to come and go, or why some people see them while others can't. Perhaps somebody is directing them—maybe God. You may believe you are the unwitting pawn of angels—that they're beings that move you around the gridiron of life without your having any say in their involvement or the outcome.

All we can say in face of these beliefs about angels is be prepared to revise all of your thinking!

To truly understand Kabbalah's take on angels, you need to understand a little more about Kabbalah.

Kabbalah is a wisdom given to humanity more than 4,000 years ago. It is a technology that shows you how to live a fulfilled life by becoming the creator or master of your own universe. Angels provide you with an infrastructure to rise to that occasion… or fall in face of it. But to really use and maximize the support that angels offer you, you'll need to understand the intelligence of angels. And that information is contained in the Zohar.

Kabbalah explains that the Bible is an encoded document; that it's really a secret language for explaining the universe. Because of this, it holds within it the wisdom of the ages. The Zohar or

the Book of Splendor, the foundation and main body of the teachings of Kabbalah, is the instruction manual that decodes the Bible. If the Bible is the first great revelation of sacred wisdom, then the Zohar is the second. It gives us precise spiritual tools for day-to-day living, explaining the laws of the universe, Creation, and the human soul.

The Zohar explains the meaning of angels as well as how and why they are here to help you. It helps make clear how to manage your personal relationships with angels. It gives you an understanding of how angels impact your every action and thought and how you, in turn, impact them. All these important aspects of angel intelligence will be shared in Part I.

Now, in truth, there are many places where you can study academic aspects of Kabbalah, and there are many books written about angels—but the purpose of life isn't to gather information. What difference does it make how much you know if you are not fulfilled? Think of it this way: you can study all the plays in football and even become an expert in the history of the game, but that won't teach you how to actually pass the ball or tackle your opponent or enjoy the game once you're out on the field. In Part II of *Angel Intelligence*, you will be introduced to many of the players—the key angels in the universe—so you'll know who your allies and opponents are. Understanding their strengths and weaknesses will help you play the game—the game of life.

But reading about angels isn't enough. You also need practical, hands-on tools. The purpose of The Kabbalah Centre and this book is to *teach you how to play the game of life*—to help you grow and become your best. In Part III, you will learn not only about the incredible power of angels but also about the technology you can use to access them directly and absorb their intelligence for your own power and growth.

Part I

Understanding Our Gleaming Universe

Kabbalah teaches that angels exist in every molecule, every thought, every breath. Indeed, our world is made of billions of angels. They are supremely powerful spiritual tools given to us to support our personal transformation. Through our thoughts and by our actions, we activate the dimension that angels inhabit and bring them to our side, both for good and for ill.

1. THE POWER OF ANGELS

Angels aren't what you may think they are. In fact, rather than angels being cute or entertaining or manipulative, Kabbalah teaches that they are an awesome force. They surround you, are inside of you, penetrate your every thought and action.

Did you know that every single thing that happens in your life is a direct result of angelic intervention? Everything!

Bite your tongue? Stub your toe? Step on the gas when you meant to hit the brake? Hammer your thumb instead of the nail? Lose your wallet? Crash your hard drive? Slip and throw out your back? Fall off a ladder?

Are these all random events? Consequences of your stupidity? Hardly. Besides, you're not that stupid! Nobody is *that* stupid! Mishaps like these that cause physical or emotional pain come from an energy force that Kabbalah calls angels. It's angels that are pushing you to make a fool of yourself.

That's the bad news.

But there's a good side to this story, too.

Just as every negative incident in your life comes from angels, so does everything positive. You don't know why you made a right turn instead of a left, but you end up on the road that leads you past the house you've always fantasized about. There it is, and it is for sale and in your price range, too. Or a friendly co-worker gets the idea to introduce you to his buddy—someone you've worked next to for years—who turns out to be a great guy. You fall in love with each other and get married. Or your boss, who seemingly doesn't know that you exist, suddenly puts your name in for a promotion, and you land that huge new account. Your life is filled with good fortune and joy.

Angels, however, don't perform magic tricks! Nor will they write your book for you or give you a raise. But they *will* be the inspiration that makes things happen in your life. It is they that can trigger the thought in your boss that says: "Hey, what about Stan? Let's give him a chance." Nothing happens without there being some unseen influence in our lives.

That unseen influence? Angels, of course.

2. THE INFRASTRUCTURE OF OUR UNIVERSE

21st century physicists have concluded that our universe operates under the jurisdiction of what they call the "Uncertainty Principle." What does this mean? It's simple. The thought we have about the direction a particle will move will affect the direction it moves. This means our actions—and even our intentions—alter and determine reality.

We can no longer rely on our old, familiar ways of thinking about life. Physicists tell us there are forces of energy-consciousness out there that influence our lives every nanosecond of every day—even though we are almost entirely unaware of them. These invisible but nonetheless powerful forces exert sway over our brains and our minds—as well as what it is we perceive as "reality."

What are these forces? Angels.

That's what the ancient wisdom of Kabbalah would call these minute, non-material packets of energy.

> *There is not even a blade of grass in the ground that does not have a supernal force upon it in the upper worlds. Everything that each does or is done to each is*

under the strength of the supernal force appointed upon it from above.

The Zohar teaches us that there is an angel for every blade of grass. Angels are the plumbing, wiring, and ductwork of the world. This statement alone has immeasurable implications: that despite the seeming randomness of our lives, there is, in fact, a system, an invisible structure to the universe.

Everything has a purpose, even if we are unable to perceive it through our limited senses. This may seem paradoxical to us. But Kabbalah teaches that when something appears paradoxical, we're probably heading in the right direction.

3. BILLIONS OF ANGELS AT YOUR FINGERTIPS

Because angels are everywhere, they provide a workforce of unimaginable numbers. There are billions upon billions of them. Here's a good way for you to grasp their infinite numbers.

The kabbalists explain that no angel ever interferes in the functioning of another angel. That's one of the basic laws of angelic being. One angel cannot have two functions, and two angels cannot share the same function. If you look closely at your little finger, you'll see that it has three joints. Each cell in each joint has an angel directing its movement! So each movement of each cell of your finger joint has its own angel, and each of these angels, in turn, has countless sub-angels—in effect, millions of molecules and cells that each have an angel, are all participating when you flex your finger.

Kabbalists pointed out thousands of years ago that the fabric of the universe is made up of three key energy forces. They refer to these forces as "columns," and the system of the universe as a Three Column System. The Right Column is the positive column. The Left Column is negative. And the Central Column is neutral. This Three Column System operates throughout the universe at every level, from the arrangement of the molecules of a snowflake to the vast array of stars beyond the Milky Way.

Since your finger joint is a member in good standing of the universe, for instance, the Three Column System applies. So every cell of your finger joint has a Right Column, a Central Column and Left Column aspect—and an angel for each aspect.

Now multiply that number of angels by three again, for the three joints in your little finger, and then by five for your five fingers, and by two for your two hands. Now picture all your fingers moving and visualize the infinite levels and sub-levels of angels required for that action. Next, imagine the complexity of your whole body, including all your thoughts, since they, too, are powered by angels.

And that's just the beginning. Imagine the thoughts of all the people in the world—endless angels stretching toward infinity. Multiply that by a hundred, a thousand, a billion, a trillion for all the animals, plants, rocks, and ocean waves in this universe. This gives you a rough sense of the immeasurable vastness of the angels' influence on our lives.

Now think of what it means to take the life of another human being. It's almost unfathomable. If such an enormous network of angelic forces is required just to move your one finger, can we even begin to conceive of the value of another life? That is why it is written in Scripture that if you save one life, it's as if you've saved the whole world. And vice versa: If you take a life, it's like destroying the world.

Now imagine the vastness and power of *the Creator Who created the whole thing...* then imagine all the angels of all the interactions and all the thoughts and all the movements of the six billion people on earth!

The sheer numbers of angels required to maintain the great engine we call life is truly awe-inspiring. This is an infinite spiritual workforce, a boundless network of packets of energy designed for a unique and singular job: to help or hinder each of us in our growth.

This is our miraculous universe, gleaming with Light.

4. ATOMIC ANGELS

Kabbalah has taught for thousands of years that angels are everywhere. But what's really amazing is that today science says the same thing. Every second of the day, millions and trillions and gazillions of particles are popping in and out of existence.

But here's what we don't realize: what science calls *particles* and what Kabbalah calls *angels* are one and the same. In fact, Kabbalah validates science. Physicists have found that space is actually teeming with megatons of energy. But Kabbalah had established this as true 2000 years ago. Science is just catching up!

Now take yourself back thousands of years. How would you explain the idea of atomic structure to simple farmers and shepherds: that there's a positive force with a positive charge called a proton, a negative force with a negative charge called an electron, and a central force of resistance called a neutron? They wouldn't just take your word for it. They'd want to see it to believe it. You wouldn't be able do it, especially without particle accelerators (you know, atom smashers), electron microscopes, and other kinds of high tech equipment used today.

The great 18th century Italian Kabbalist Moses Chaim Luzatto tells us that we cannot see the invisible world with our five

senses. And because the kabbalists 2000 years ago couldn't explain protons, electrons, and neutrons—or positive force, negative force, and resistance—they depicted this energy as a winged cherub! The right wing is the positive charge. The left wing is the negative charge. And the body in between is the neutron—the free will, the force of resistance. It's the Three Column System I mentioned a few pages ago.

These images and metaphors have been given to us to help us understand the concept. That's how the whole idea of the winged-cherub-cum-angel came into existence. This depiction of an "angel" makes it easier for us to conceptualize the parts of reality we cannot see.

Unfortunately, many of us still take the image literally, and that's what can cause confusion. When someone talks of a two-winged, haloed creature floating around in ethereal robes, skeptics find it hard to swallow. And in truth, it can sound ridiculous. But when scientists tell us that the empty space all around us is hopping with unseen energy, when they call these packets of energy atoms or electrons or protons or leptons or neutrinos or quarks, we accept their explanation. We say, "Oh yeah, atomic energy is everywhere," even though we can't actually touch or see *these* particles either.

When kabbalists tell us that the universe is alive with angelic energy, when they explain that angelic energy is everywhere, they're saying the same thing as the physicists. It's only the language that has us confused.

We're all made up of atoms. Those are the particles that give us existence. But atoms are not physical; really maybe less than one percent of the atom is physical. The latest findings in physics tell us that atoms are really nothing but vibrations. These vibrations create the illusion of physicality. Atoms are really just energy. Atoms are the angels.

And most people—the 98 percent of us who are believers—have an innate feeling that there is some kind of angelic force out there. We can feel it although we may have a hard time truly explaining it... until now.

5. CREATING ANGELS

Where do angels come from? Some, like your Guardian Angel, the Archangels, and Satan (the Angel of Death) are a permanent part of our Light-filled universe. I'll introduce them to you in Part II of this book. But for now, let's look at the ones that we create on our own! These we call temporary angels.

Yes, that's right. We make our own angels.

The great Kabbalist, Rav Isaac Luria (the Ari) lived in the hills of northern Israel in the 16th century. It is said he was so spiritually developed he could read a person's entire life simply by looking at his forehead.

The Ari never wrote a single word during his time on this Earth, but his influence was so profound that his teachings, recorded by his students after his death, filled many books known as the *Kitve HaAri,* or the *Writings of the Ari*.

Rav Isaac Luria taught that temporary angels are energy forces, both good and bad, which are formed by our words, deeds, and intentions.

There are angels that belong to Asiyah or the World of Action, and they are being created by deeds solely, independent of our intentions.

There are angels from Beri'ah, the World of Creation, and they are beings made from the intention of the person and from the thought... the mind.

Kabbalists tell us that every single action in which we engage, every thought that flits though our brain, every word we utter, creates a positive or a negative angel. These angels pop right into existence in a steady stream.

While our lives may appear to be a *random sequence* of both good and challenging events, this is not the case. Only our lack of awareness makes life seem arbitrary to us. Ultimately, we have responsibility for our lives. Angels merely help us manifest what we have earned, whether it's a computer hard drive crash or a wonderful husband.

What can we learn from this? A couple of really important lessons.

6. THE POWER OF NEGATIVE AND POSITIVE ANGELS

If you jump off a cliff, no matter who you are, the law of gravity is going to take effect, whether you understand it or not. Most likely you're going to suffer some aches and pains (if not worse) as a result! Similarly, angels are packets of energy that affect you whether or not you are conscious of their influence. Even if you don't "believe" in them, they will still impact your life. Angels are not just passive entities. They exert energy.

So here's the first lesson: Watch out! Every harsh word, every negative action toward another human being, and every egocentric impulse spawns a negative angel that blocks and hinders you.

You cursed or were scornful? You slept with your best friend's wife? You cheated a customer? You screamed at your child? You snubbed an old friend? Bam! You just brought negative angels into existence.

So when bad things happen, you may want to shake your fists and rail, "God, you've caused this tragedy to happen to me!" But that's not the way the universe actually works. The negative angels we create are the cause of chaos and destruction. They

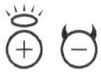

cover our eyes when we're driving so we just don't "see" the car in the next lane as we prepare to move over.

They play havoc with relationships. Picture the times you try to communicate with someone, but it's hopeless. The harder you work to make him/her understand you, the more confusing it all gets. You keep thinking that just one more statement, one further clarification will straighten it all out, but the other person just becomes angrier or more distant. You wonder if you're even speaking the same language.

Negative angels blind you. You put your keys on your desk, but they disappear. You search all over, opening drawers and shuffling papers, but the keys are nowhere to be found. So you go back to where they should have been in the first place, only now you find them. How could the keys be on your desk now when they weren't just a minute ago? Are you losing your mind?

No, the truth is you're experiencing an angelic existence. Somewhere along the line, through word or deed, you created a negative angel and now it's playing with your mind, wasting your time, and causing you frustration and grief. Unfortunately, that negative force is just doing its job.

Now you can see why our negative traits like anger, jealousy, guilt, shame, aggressiveness, fear, and depression aren't simply undesirable or unpleasant moods. They're much worse because they're toxic to our bodies and our souls. They are to be guarded

against as vigilantly as we would defend ourselves from any virus or poison that infiltrates our bodies.

So here's the second lesson: Kabbalah teaches that no matter where we are, no matter what we have done, we can also create positive angels that bless and support our growth.

You offered a kind word and a helping hand? You took care of your old, sick aunt without any expectation of reward? You let another driver merge in front of you? You admitted to a personal failing and resolved to correct it? You decided not to react when your mother pushed your buttons? Boom! You bring positive angels into your life.

The positive is just as real as the negative. When you build up people instead of knocking them down, when you share instead of taking for yourself alone, when you behave proactively instead of reactively, when you become the cause in your life and not just the effect of external forces, positive angels are born.

When you stop to think about how many of these forces are popping in and out of existence in any one second, you start to realize just how much power you have to create your own reality.

Kabbalah explains this process as "reverse marionettes." When we watch a puppet show, we usually imagine the puppeteers manipulating the strings above the curtain, making the marionettes talk, run, sing, and jump on the stage below. But in the kabbalistic universe, the puppets—that is, you and I—control the strings. Our actions here on Earth move Heaven above.

The Creator set up this world so that we could be empowered and in charge. He created it so that we can take responsibility for our lives and our choices.

Until now, you were probably unaware of this awesome power. Now that you know you have it, what are you going to do with it?

7. WHY DO ANGELS EXIST, ANYWAY?

Why do angels exist? I'll answer that question with another question. Why do we exist? What is the purpose of our lives?

Kabbalah teaches that our purpose is to find fulfillment and become the master of our own universe. As we complete our individual correction (*tikkun*), which drove us to inhabit this world in the first place, we are able to return to our original Godlike state.

What does this mean? It may be helpful to think about life in terms of a football game. To become the number one player or team in your football league—to reach fulfillment—means that within the rules of the game, you have risen above many obstacles: the opposing team, gravity, the condition of the field, the weather, the unpredictable bounce of the football. These are all factors that push you to become your best in the game of football. Indeed, to reach fulfillment and become your best, you have to rise above the quirky challenges and difficulties of life.

Why do we all yearn to reach fulfillment?

According to kabbalistic wisdom, this yearning hearkens back to a time before time—to the Endless World when we were all one with the Light of the Creator, the infinite Force of sharing and giving and fulfillment. The Light is the energy of the

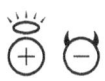

universe—*the Lightforce of the Creator*. But because sharing requires a container to hold the beneficence of that sharing, the Light created an infinite receiver. In Kabbalah, we call this receiver the Vessel, and its purpose was to receive all that the Light had to share. The Vessel wanted everything the Light had to offer, the Light gave it everything it had, and for a while there was complete and perfect harmony.

But that changed. Along with all of the Creator's other gifts, the Vessel had also absorbed the Light's sharing nature, so it, too, wanted to share. But the Light could not receive, only give. Since the Creator's only intention was to please the Vessel, the Creator withdrew the Light, thus initiating the process that led to the creation of our physical universe—the Big Bang, time, space, motion, all the souls of humanity—a domain in which we can be the cause and creator of our own destiny, where we have a chance to share, where we can exhibit our Godly nature and thus connect back to the Light, back to the original fulfillment of endless Light.

All of us are offspring of that original Vessel. We have created a game whereby we take up bodies, forget our true Godlike nature, and come to a realm of challenges and difficulties, chaos and suffering, in order to overcome, share, create, resolve, and then work our way back toward the Light. *We do this because this is how we find true fulfillment.* Along the way, we go through confusion and doubt in order to discover clarity and certainty, through indecision and ambivalence in order to decide and care, and through struggle and pain so that we can

rise above and overcome our limitations. That is the game and the reason why we play. We do this because we want to reveal the Light within us.

There is an intelligent structure in our universe—of positive and negative forces and angels in our universe—that is here to help or challenge us in our quest to reconnect with whom we were and are and should be, and to the fulfillment we seek from the Light of the Creator. *This is the secret that explains why angels exist.* They act as a wiring system to help us link up to the Creator and to the non-physical universe. Angels are our bridge to the Creator. They are the infrastructure of our universe, an infrastructure that we can ultimately control.

Angels help us become the cause, the creators of our own destinies. They provide a system of total responsibility. When we understand the nature of angel intelligence, we can embrace completely the concept that nothing in the universe is random—that we cause everything that happens in our lives.

This is both a daunting and an empowering thought. On the one hand, we can say, "Wow! I can totally make my life what I want it to be—for good or for bad." Or we can say, "Wow! This is a major responsibility we're talking about here!" Both of these thoughts are true, by the way.

So why do we need this wiring system to help us connect to the Creator? Why can't we just connect to the Light directly?

8. THE WIRING SYSTEM

Kabbalah teaches, and Superstring Theory physicists agree, that the world is a vast spiritual place. What appears permanent—just knock on a table—is mere appearance, a grand illusion provided by billions of vibrating atoms. Remember, scientists have confirmed that the atom, and therefore matter itself, is mostly empty space, even if it seems solid to our eyes. Yes, this "real world" of headphones and hamburgers, of televisions and toothbrushes, which we see, hear, taste, touch, and smell, is not the whole picture. In fact, it's more like a momentary snapshot that gives very little sense of the larger picture—it's just one percent of the real story, of the true reality.

I like to think of this so-called "real world" as the World of Questions—questions to which we feel we get no answers. And we certainly have so many profound questions: We want to know why our prayers go unanswered, why we suffer, what's the meaning of our lives, what the future holds, why we die. This World of Questions—our physical world—is one of darkness, pain, aggression, fear, anger, sickness, and chaos.

The much larger reality—the World of Answers—emanates from the Creator. This is the pure, blazing, blinding Light. This is the domain where true fulfillment resides, the domain that is spiritual and most often hidden from our view. According to

Kabbalah, Heaven is not a *place* but a connection to this World of Answers. This is the level of all intelligence, all answers, all fulfillment. This is the 99 Percent World.

So there are two worlds: the world of Light, or answers, and the world of senses, or questions. How do we pass from one realm to the other? **The angels are our ticket. They provide a transportation system, allowing movement between these two spheres.**

Why can't we access the World of Answers directly, without these intermediaries?

It may be helpful to consider this in terms of electricity. Even if you wanted to, you couldn't plug your toaster into a nuclear power plant. The toaster itself would become toast in a flash. To harness the enormous invisible power generated at such a facility, we've had to build wires, cables, and transformers housed in transmitting stations. These mechanisms step down the colossal surge of current and deliver it into our homes in usable form so a plug goes neatly into the outlet and ding! our toast comes out a nice golden brown.

Angels are those wires, cables, and transformers on a spiritual level. They are the interface between us and the World of Answers. They are transmitting stations—conduits for the Light, distributing its titanic blaze of energy into tiny packets we can access and use.

Each angel is a single wire in the computer of the universe. Each has an individual identity, each is a singular work unit of energy, and each is a channel for the Lightforce of God. Angels are there for us to harness: to help us in our jobs, in our relationships, in our spiritual development.

But how?

How do we access them, especially since they're invisible to us?

9. WHY CAN'T WE SEE THEM?

The Zohar explains that if we were to gaze fully upon the World of Answers and the vast cosmic infrastructure of angels of which it is composed, we would lose our mind. The fact is, we don't have the capacity to see angels because we, who are made of flesh and blood, are immersed in the world of the senses. The World of Questions puts a tightly limiting and restrictive frame around our perceptions.

Besides, the invisibility of the angelic world serves as a kind of protection for us. We don't want to see angels, because to do so would mean confronting the full truth of our selves. We would come face to face with our *tikkun* (our correction), with what the sages have brutally called "the filth" of our nature—the layers and layers of accumulated negativity, built up over this and many past lifetimes from every time we acted egocentrically, every time we were insensitive, every time we hurt someone. All of these selfish acts remain in our souls as layers of, well, garbage.

The invisibility of the angelic world serves as a kind of protection for us.

In the end, it is the angels who determine what we see and what we don't. And we always see exactly what we need to. Our perceptions reflect the state of our consciousness. As we grow spiritually and expand our Vessel, the spiritual world, our gleaming universe of Light reveals itself to us.

All we need to do is throw open the windows!

10. WINDOWS AND BLINDS

Okay, read this carefully, because now I'm going to blow your mind. Despite what most of us believe, *there is no such thing as evil*. Yes, that's what I said. In fact, I'm going to climb further out on this limb to state emphatically that *there's no such thing as a demon*!

But what does that really mean?

To put it simply, "angel" is another word for energy. And "demon" is another word for something that blocks energy. That's all there is to it!

Imagine the World of Answers—the world of Light. It's a glorious place, but none of us are there. No, we live in the physical world, surrounded by a thick curtain or wall that blocks out this Light. Literally, we're more or less in the dark. And that's too bad, because:

- Light is happiness; darkness is sadness.
- Light is certainty; darkness is doubt.
- Light is courage; darkness is fear.
- Light is clarity; darkness confusion.
- Light is peace; darkness is chaos.
- Light is love; darkness is hatred.

- Light is joyfulness; darkness is rage.
- Light is wholeness; darkness disease.
- Light is immortality; darkness is death.

Now think of an angel as a window into the World of Answers. It's a window that lets the Light into our dark physical reality.

What's a demon? It's really just a blackout curtain, a blind. When it covers the window, the Light seems to go out and we are plunged into gloom.

The demonic force, otherwise known as evil, is not merely the absence of Light but a powerful void. This darkness is a force to be reckoned with. It is a polarity—the opposite of the force of Light. It has its own gravity—it sucks you in like a black hole.

But that demonic force is *an absence we create ourselves by pulling down the blinds*. With each unkind act, intolerant word, curse, or indulgence, we cover the windows that bring the Light into our lives. With every self-absorbed act, we create a negative angel—a demon, if you will—and another curtain separates us even further from the Light. The more negativity we project out into the world, the greater the number of blinds we put up on the windows in our lives. And conversely, the more good we do, the more windows are opened, and the more Light we let in.

Of course, there are infinite shades of gray between the polar opposites of light and dark. So depending on how many blinds

you've hung up in your life and how many windows you've opened to let in the Light, depending on how many negative and positive angels surround you—that's the state of your life, the state of your mind, the state of your existence, the state of your being. These are the conditions that prevail in your life at any given moment.

So ask yourself: How many demons do I have blocking the Light? How many windows have I thrown open?

11. TEENAGE WASTELAND

When we are floating blissfully in the womb, we know everything—the past and the future. We are part of the Light.

Then we are born.

At that moment, our personal Guardian Angel (we'll talk about him or her in Part II) taps us on the lip. (Evidence of this angelic touch can be seen in the little vertical groove between our nose and mouth.) With that touch, we forget almost everything we know. But at birth we're innocent, unstained by the negativity that awaits, so lots of windows are still open in our lives to nurture and support us.

When a baby is born, there are certain positive angels around her that provide windows to the World of Answers. These include the love, nurturing, and the stimulation she gets from her parents, grandparents, and other loved ones.

Think about it. A child derives so much pleasure just from playing with toy blocks! Can you imagine a 45-year-old woman spending her days building towers out of blocks or playing with her fingers or talking to socks? She'd either be bored out of her gourd or we'd think her quite mad!

The esteemed Kabbalist Rav Ashlag explains that these windows to the Light help young children grow. That's why they derive pleasure so easily. That joy is the Light, and actually, it's the Light that makes children grow. Their windows are open and they're letting the sun shine in!

But what happens when a child reaches puberty? When teenagers step into the world of adulthood, they suddenly have the power to open more windows—or to hang blinds.

So now that you're thinking about it, ask yourself, these simple questions: When do all of our bad habits begin? When do we start swearing and cursing? When do we lose our temper and storm out of rooms, slamming doors with bone-rattling finality? When do we behave as if the universe were orbiting around us? When are we lured by the quick pleasures of sex, drugs, and rock and roll?

Puberty is the time when we start actively putting up shutters, shades, drapes, curtains, and blinds. That's why as teenagers and adults, we find it so hard to derive the same kind of pleasure we reveled in as kids.

Because, in truth, puberty is the age of responsibility. That's when we become accountable.

12. IT'S ALL IN YOUR HANDS

Here's the good news about being accountable. Remember the expression: "Power to the people"? Well, you've got the power, my friend. You're responsible for everything that happens in your life—and for creating the angels that surround you.

What does this ancient insight mean to your life today? A lot. Angels are the agents of your karma, of cause and effect. They are packets of energy drawn down by your words and deeds. And they are a network of energy you can ask to help you. (More on how to do that in Part III.)

According to the Zohar, when you hurt someone, break a trust, or act cruelly, you pull down the blinds and attract destructive angels to you. But acts of sharing and loving kindness create an affinity with the positive aspects of energy, attracting positive angels and Light.

Although these positive and negative forces of energy existed long before you entered the theater of this world, they remain dormant, in a state of suspended animation, until the moment you create a suitable garment or vehicle through which they can reveal themselves. When you occupy yourself with spirituality, prayer, meditation, and sharing, the very breath that leaves your

mouth becomes what the Ari called "a chariot"—a vehicle for positive angels.

This means you are directly responsible for the angels in your life, that is, which angels will come in contact with you. You have total responsibility. **You are linked to every cell in the world. You are significant beyond your wildest imagining. You create angels!**

13. TOUCHED BY AN ANGEL

How do you know when you've encountered an angel? The Zohar tells the story of Abraham, who underwent the ritual of circumcision at an extremely advanced age. Not surprisingly, he suffered greatly. To ease his pain, God sent Abraham "three visible angels to inquire of his well-being." Even though they were angels, or pure energy, they came to Abraham in physical form to communicate with him.

> *He certainly did see them because they came to earth in the image of men. And it should not be hard for you to understand because they are definitely holy spirits. But when they come down to this world, they enclothe themselves with the air and the elements of covering and enveloping, until they appear to people exactly in their image.*

Kabbalah tells us that angels exist in our midst. The crazy opportunity that suddenly falls into our lap; the disturbance that shakes us up; the inspiration to create a painting or write a song; the sudden urge to weep; the overwhelming feeling of love; the sense of awe as the sun sets into the ocean or behind towering mountains: these are all angels clothed in the elements of this world.

Who is that mysterious stranger who bumps into you, pushing you aside at the very instant a car careens onto the curb, thus saving your life? Who is the old woman with the warm smile sitting next to you in the restaurant who whispers to you that your baby is "a gift from God"? Who is the teacher who recognizes your gifts when no one else does, opening the door to a future you could never have imagined?

In contrast, who is the deranged person who curses you on the street? The conniving salesman who seeks to cheat you? The jealous co-worker whose lies jeopardize your job?

These might be ordinary people. Or they could be angels appearing "exactly in . . . [your] image," saving your life or helping you in other, more paradoxical ways to take the next step in your spiritual evolution.

The truth is you can usually sense when a positive angel steps into your life. Suddenly a flash of inspiration strikes and some intractable problem you've been struggling with is solved. This happens in mysterious ways—or at least in ways that appear mysterious.

Our perception is a function of our consciousness. As our awareness grows, so will our sensitivity to angels. As we attain higher consciousness, we can read the clues and decode the messages from the World of Answers more readily. We will see what is now invisible.

Reality is a mirror. We get back in the form of angels exactly what we put out. And once formed, these angels help or hinder us, curse or bless us.

So how do we create positive angels in our life? The next few chapters will provide some pointers.

14. CREATING ANGELS: CHOOSING YOUR WORDS

We rarely notice as our words—love songs, polite banter, idle chatter, spiteful gossip, scathing criticism—exit our mouths and take their place in the global cacophony. But we should be careful. Those words so casually slipping from our lips give birth to angels.

We live in a universe where invisible energies are at work. When you speak well of someone, a positive angel sings your praises in your boss's ear. But delicious gossip kills more swiftly than a double bacon cheese burger, a large order of fries, and a pack of cigarettes. Envious words corrode the soul, damaging *you* as well as the object of your jealousy, pulling you further into negativity. When you speak ill of others, indulging in what Aramaic refers to as *lashon hara* (giving voice to your pessimistic imaginings and limiting beliefs), a negative spiritual force grows, and its tentacles wrap tightly around your arms and legs.

Speaking hurtfully may be the conversational norm in our society, and if so, that is tragic. Every disparaging word creates a negative angel. When we denigrate another person in speech, we are also destroying ourselves; a negative angel takes up residence within us, thwarting our spiritual growth.

Remember that proverb: "If you don't have something good to say, don't say anything at all"? It's an old outdated cliché, right? Wrong! It may be old, but it isn't outdated. **It is a scientific description of the angelic wiring of the universe.** If we want the blessings of positive angels, we can no longer let our thoughtless mouths run on with no one at the voice box.

15. CREATING ANGELS: CHOOSING YOUR ACTIONS

Think about it. If you really, truly understood that every kind deed creates a positive force in your life while every unkind one creates a negative force, you'd change your ways in a second. Who wouldn't? You'd be stupid not to.

It's like that television character, Earl Hickey, in the hit comedy *My Name Is Earl*. Immediately after winning $100,000 in the lottery, this petty thief, liar, and all-around shiftless no-goodnik, is hit by a car and loses his winning ticket. Laid up in the hospital, he watches a TV show where he learns the basic rule of karma: what goes around, comes around. And so he draws up a long list of all of the people he has wronged in his many years of malicious mischief and then methodically goes about trying to make amends with each and every one of them. Usually his efforts not only help the person he wronged but also lead to other unexpected positive results that no one could have predicted. After all, his hurtful actions, like pebbles dropped in a still lake, he also had rippling unforeseen negative consequences.

There is reason for hope. Once we reach a certain level of awareness, even our Negative Angel becomes helpful. Earl Hickey is a good example, but he's a fictional character. Think

of a felon, a gangster who was incarcerated but later becomes a counselor for prisoners or at-risk youth. He has taken the darkest part of his life and transformed it into positivity. Think of a drug addict who becomes clean and sober and then acts as a sponsor for others who are struggling with this addiction. Think of a tsunami victim who, in the midst of her own suffering, helps others to higher ground.

We all come into this world with both garbage and gifts. Each of us has his own specific path, but we share a general life mission. Our task is to transform our garbage and connect to our gifts. And one of the best ways to do that is through positive actions.

16. CREATING ANGELS: CHOOSING YOUR FRIENDS

According to Kabbalah, the spiritual influence that we exert is so great that we can cause our friends to create good and bad angels in their own lives, and they return the favor! Therefore, it is extremely important that we choose our friends wisely. To become better people ourselves, we must spend time with better people.

Sadly, we tend to live rather randomly. Just like the words that flow unexamined from our mouths, people come and go in our lives. It's like . . . *whatever*—or more accurately . . . *whoever*.

You run into a group and someone latches onto you, or you latch on to someone else. You've got nothing better to do, and no one better to do it with, so you hang out. Out of loneliness, you may befriend people who instill doubt in your life. Or you may surround yourself with negative people who exude destructive energies. You may even think you have no choice because you "want to be nice."

But being "nice" can be spiritual suicide. Kabbalah teaches us that human dignity is important, but if you are "nice and polite" with someone who is negative or has an agenda for you, it's a recipe for disaster. Why? Because it causes you to create a

negative angel *in your own life*! For instance, if you're dating a girl who doesn't really like you but is just stringing you along until someone "better" comes along, you'll create a negative angel that will play havoc with your life. Better not to be with her at all than to put yourself in such a self-defeating situation!

You don't owe negative individuals like this anything. If they try to convince you that you do, they are not your friends. So-called friends who have a hidden agenda, who take what they can from you or bring you down with negative energy, prompt you to create negative angels. You must wish these "friends" well and move on. Quickly.

Why does Kabbalah teach that it is *you* who creates the negative angels and not these nefarious "friends"? Because we asked for, created, and live in a world of total responsibility. If our life is not positive, it's only because we've done something to create the negativity. We are not victims; we are the cause of our own reality! Uncomfortable as it might be, we can—and must—choose to step away from people who are hurtful to us.

True friends have no agenda. They care for your growth and well-being. They cause you to create good angels in your life by making the wise choice to be their friend.

The lesson of the temporary angels, the ones you create with your words and actions, is one of total responsibility.

17. CREATING ANGELS: USING YOUR POWER

At the moment we pass on, as our lives flash before our eyes, our agendas dissolve, negativity evaporates, and love comes to the fore. It is then that we have the clarity of an angel. We see what we did right and what we did wrong. We recognize that we might have to come back to correct a personal failing, that perhaps we missed our correction by just a hair. We grasp the truth that when we hate someone, we are the ones who get hurt. And we understand cause and effect with blazing obviousness.

But we don't have to wait until we die. We can have clarity and become law-abiding citizens of the universe now.

The paradox is that on the one hand, we require the help of angels. We need them for assistance, for protection and blessings. On the other hand, we are exceedingly powerful. Indeed, it has been said that humans are potent beings busy believing they are ants. Angels are powerful in how they govern our lives, but we are more powerful in how we govern their functions!

18. FREE WILL AND DOUBT

Angels are not like humans. They do their jobs without a lot of internal conflict. We, on the other hand, wander around in a state of confusion and ambivalence. We mull it over. To the gym or to the doughnut shop? By freeway or using side streets? Finish the work or turn on the TV? Tell the cashier she made a mistake or keep the extra money? Call my sister or read a book? Do I lie or tell the truth? Do I want chocolate or vanilla? Should I take that wallet that was dropped there—no one will see—or should I leave it in case its owner returns?

Okay, these examples range from the sublime to the ridiculous, but we are creatures who rarely seem certain about what we should do unless our survival is threatened—and even then we may be wracked with doubts. Our free will—the opportunity to choose our actions—is the basis for our confusion, but it is also the source of our spiritual correction.

Think again about that game of football. You may have a great coach and a series of plays worked out, but once you're on the field, you're on your own. You create the game with your own actions in relation to those of your team and the opposing team, in relation to the conditions on the field, in relation to the crowd. Every choice you make, every turn to the right or left, creates a whole new dynamic, which creates a whole new game. You

could be pushed back to the twenty-yard line but suddenly see a great window to your receiver and pass for a touchdown. Similarly, every choice you make in the game of life can move you closer to your goal of fulfillment. But without free will, you could never earn the Light you came here to receive because you would be powerless to make those choices.

Kabbalah tells us that we derive no fulfillment from anything just handed over to us, anything we haven't earned. Though a million lottery ticket buyers would beg to differ, we didn't come to this world for a free lunch. The winners would tell you a different story, however. Too many of their lives suddenly became nightmares following that large infusion of unearned cash. We came into this physical world to become the *Cause* in our lives—the boss—and not the *Effect*. We came down to the World of Questions to take responsibility and figure out the "right" answers for ourselves.

How do we allow our positive angels to flourish? Remember, angels are guided by us. Our mission is to clear out the negativity before it takes hold. Our most important work is to transform the negative aspects of our soul in order to open windows to the Light. When we exert free will to make good choices, we reach toward fulfillment and the true purpose of our lives.

19. DO ANGELS HAVE FREE WILL?

Humans are creatures of doubt, but not angels. They have no doubt. They do not spend time trying to find their "real" selves. They don't become confused. They don't see one job or relationship as simply a stepping stone to a better one. Angels don't have to earn their fulfillment. Angels are content to accomplish their specific mission.

Does this mean angels don't have free will? Like so much else that is paradoxical about angels, they do and they don't. They have the power of choice just as we do, but they also enjoy the advantage of perspective. They don't have curtains, so they know what is Light and what is darkness. After all, if you could see the road to fulfillment, why would you take another way? Angels are so close to the Light that they see the ramifications of their actions.

We humans are different from the angels. In the game of life we play down here, we must factor in the curtains, and especially the veil of time. Time is a challenge because *time is the veil between cause and effect!*

20. THE VEIL OF TIME

We live in a cause-and-effect world. Nothing is random, nothing "just happens." There are no coincidences or accidents. It just seems to our limited senses as if there are. Why do we lose sight of the truth?

The answer is *time*.

If someone smashed you on the head with a Louisville Slugger whenever you descended into egocentric behavior, would you continue to behave badly? Of course not. But time serves to confuse the issue. If you hurt somebody today—say, you steal a watch in New York and no one catches you—you may believe that you got away with it. But sometime later, perhaps on another continent, something of equal value will be taken from you. Since the consequence of your original action (stealing the watch) shows up in a different time and place, you may not recognize the machinery of cause and effect.

Angels don't live on the illusory stage set of time and are therefore not confused by it. Although time keeps us humans from perceiving cause and effect, it also allows us to enjoy free will—which, unfortunately, is a privilege we often abuse. And that is the nature and the limitation of our physical senses.

But the good news is that free will gives us the power to overcome our nature. When we decide to oppose our egocentric character—in effect, rising to a more angelic state—we are rewarded, not because we've been hit upside the head with a baseball bat but because we have chosen well.

And these positive effects are cumulative, not just for us as individuals but for humankind as a whole.

21. A FISH DOESN'T KNOW IT'S IN WATER

A fish doesn't know it's swimming around in the water because it has no point of reference. But just take a fish out of its environment for a moment and then plop it back in the tank. The water will be exactly the same, but the fish's "appreciation" of it will be changed forever.

I'd like you to think about how this metaphor might work in your life. I hope you have the experience of rising up out of the water of your life, shifting the paradigm, breaking the frame, and sensing the invisible energies that form the infrastructure of the universe. There are many kabbalistic tools for doing so, as you will find in Part III of this book. My goal is to help you realize that beyond the walls, carpets, pictures, and books in our environment, we are bathed in an invisible atmosphere of angelic energy. Every moment of our lives, we are bombarded with positive and negative energy, surrounded by positive and negative angels. They have an impact on our health, happiness, sense of well-being, success, and failure.

When our consciousness grows and our positive actions proliferate, we create more positive angels to help us along on the right path. And it is by our choices that we determine which angels will act as our support staff.

22. JACOB'S GLEAMING UNIVERSE

And so Jacob travels to the land of Charan. It is a journey of escape, a flight from his brother, Esau.

Along the way he grows tired, and stops to rest beneath a glittering dome of stars. Drifting off to sleep, Jacob dreams a dream.

In the dream, a ladder is set up upon the earth, with its top reaching Heaven itself. And upon the rungs of this celestial ladder, the angels of God are ascending and descending.

He is mesmerized by the angels. Then God reveals Himself. He promises Jacob protection, He promises him a multitude of descendants, and He promises him the land he lies upon as a gift.

This holy spot in which the dream of Jacob's ladder is dreamt came to be called "Beit-El" or House of God. The spot is an aperture to the Higher World. It is the Gate of Heaven, an opening to the spiritual universe and fulfillment.

Jacob's dream of angels ascending and descending the ladder is not just a biblical story but a description of the invisible architecture and infrastructure of the universe available to us. Like Jacob, when a person truly understands and is in sync with the system of this world—a system through which the Creator reveals His gifts to us—we can have it all: *everything that the Creator promised to Jacob.*

Kabbalah tells us that Jacob attained a level of complete prophesy. He tapped into the whole picture of the universe—past, present, and future.

Part II

It Helps to Know the Players

Some angels come and go, while others are always there for us. There are anonymous angels and angels with names. Each of us has at least two personal angels—our Guardian Angel and our Negative Angel, our Opponent. And there are other angels who have been here from the beginning. Eternal, they were present at the dawn of Creation and will continue to be present until eternity. They are everlasting angels, permanent spiritual intelligences who can be counted on when we call.

Every permanent angel has a name. What's more, *only* permanent angels have names. Their names are like their telephone numbers. When we meditate on or say their names, we can bring these angels to our side. There are millions of permanent angels, each with a name, each with a singular form of energy. Why should we learn about some of them?

Think back now to that football game. Before you run out onto the field, it helps to know the plays, the rules, your strengths and weaknesses, your opponents' strengths and weaknesses, and where the goal line is. The better you understand these variables, the more effective your efforts will be. Indeed, if no one teaches you the rules, you could be running the wrong way altogether and scoring for the opposing team!

In these next pages, I'm going to introduce you to many of the players—the key angels in the universe—so you'll understand your allies and opponents and can better play the game using angel intelligence.

23. ANGELS ON YOUR SHOULDER

How can you best understand the existence of positive and negative forces of energy—positive and negative angels—in your life? Remember, you cannot perceive the invisible world with your five senses. Again, Kabbalah provides us with metaphors to help us.

> *For we have learned that assuredly man has two angels, who are messengers that join him from Above. One is on his right and the other on his left. They observe man in everything he does. They are called "the Good Inclination" and "the Evil Inclination."*

Of course, you've seen these images in movies, cartoons, or even TV commercials! Someone is on the horns of a moral dilemma—from sneaking another piece of pie to betraying his wife—struggling with the conflicting forces of good and evil. A good angel is seated on his right shoulder, whispering in his ear, urging him to act wisely. "Be careful," the angel warns. "You know how to behave. Do the right thing." A devil sits on the person's left shoulder, pressing him in the other direction: "Who's it gonna hurt? Everybody's doing it. Just one time. No one will find out."

Kabbalah teaches us that these are not temporary angels that pop in and out of existence, depending on our behavior and thoughts. No, when we were born, these two angels were immediately allocated to us. They are a permanent part of our lives. The good angel is our Guardian Angel. He stands on the right side, but remains dormant until we reach puberty. This Guardian Angel flourishes in the Light. The Negative Angel, our Opponent, who sits on our left, is part of the universal force of Satan, not the pitchfork-wielding red-suited fellow but the force we referred to earlier, the absence of Light.

Everyone begins life with these angels in balance. No matter how heavy the burden of our past negative actions, no matter how many layers of egocentric behavior we must shed, no matter how much "garbage" our soul has accumulated, we all have gifts as well as negativity. Every astrological sign has its positive and negative characteristics and, as the Zohar teaches, every organ in our bodies contains both good and bad.

Each of us has negative and positive angels in our very cells, waging war for our destiny. These two forces either obstruct or encourage our spiritual development. When we have the Desire to Receive for the Self Alone, when we allow our ego to overtake us, this gives the advantage to our Opponent. But when we activate and practice our desire for selfless sharing, our Guardian Angel is making its influence known.

Science has taught us the difference between the left brain and the right brain. The right brain is our instinctual and emotional hemisphere. The left brain is our rational and logical hemisphere. The left brain is the hemisphere of the five senses, the repository of our history, the scrapbook of all we have been taught. It is connected to the past. It blocks us from spirituality by its focus on analysis, calculation, and memory. It separates us from our Guardian Angel. The right brain gives us the experience of a sixth sense, telepathy, and spirituality. And it is the location where we forge our connection to our Guardian Angel.

24. MEET YOUR GUARDIAN ANGEL

Your Guardian Angel escorted your soul into this world at birth and will leave you when you die. This angel travels alongside you throughout the journey of your life. He creates tests to help you elevate. He pokes you if you're veering off the path. He's your teacher, friend, and gadfly—your spiritual partner in this life.

In fact, I like to think of guardian angels as our personal elevators. If we live in this physical realm, we don't have answers, only questions. Many blinds and curtains cover the Light and keep us from the truth. We must gain access to the World of Answers to find out why we're here. When we elevate ourselves to a higher spiritual plane, those questions disappear, dissolving into the splendor of our gleaming universe, which is filled with Light.

Our personal Guardian Angel is our elevator to this higher place. The more we open ourselves to his influence, the higher we can rise.

Guardian angels help us attain levels that we can't achieve on our own merits. They make the connections. They use their influence to intercede on our behalf. They act as our attorney, negotiating to bring us the best deal for our spiritual growth. They help us open the windows.

Whenever you are going through a hard time, whenever you are questioning, you can reach out to your Guardian Angel for answers. In Part III, I'll explain how you can connect to this force for goodness in your life.

Look to your right shoulder. Know that there is a positive angel there, even though you may not see him, and he presides over mercy.

Look to your left. There is a Negative Angel there, and he presides over judgment.

25. NOW MEET YOUR OPPONENT

Just as a magnetic pole pulls all compasses to true north, your Negative Angel, your Opponent, pulls you toward destructive behavior. His mission is to feed off your negativity and consume as much of your energy as he can. He convinces you to do wrong, to close the curtains to the Light. Born of the Desire to Receive for the Self Alone, he pressures you to indulge in reactive and egocentric acts, thus generating even more negative energy. Your Opponent is an enemy perched inside you, whispering in your ear, prompting you to utter spiteful words, make destructive choices, and live in a fog of self-centeredness, jealousy, and insecurity—in short, to pull down the shades and shut out the Light.

Your Opponent's job is to tell you that you're not responsible, to have you believe that life is random and full of coincidence, to encourage you to blame others for your fate, to make you doubt the existence of angels, when they comprise the true technology of life.

When you resist automatic and reactive behavior, you begin to strike a blow for freedom from your default nature. In this effort to exert your free will, your Guardian Angel is available to help when you call upon him.

Despite his inherently destructive nature, your Opponent actually plays a crucial role in your spiritual development and your journey toward fulfillment. Think of that football game again. The opposing team creates a force against which you must push in order to become your best. What actions will you take in face of this resistance? How will you confront the opposition? Some decisions may bring forward movement and others may lead to even more negativity, causing you to work that much harder to regain lost ground and overcome new obstacles in your path.

Your Opponent actually helps you understand your strengths and weaknesses. Indeed, knowing your Opponent makes it easier for you to know yourself, which, in turn, can help you maximize your merits as you minimize your shortcomings. Remember, kabbalistic wisdom tells us that we derive no fulfillment from anything we don't earn. Your Opponent makes you work hard toward your own betterment.

But there is urgency to this process. We are each granted a defined period of time in this world to cleanse ourselves of negative energy. The clock of *tikkun* is ticking down. Every time we give in to our Opponent, every time we believe the excuses he gives us, we lose time. When the cosmic hourglass registers that there is too little time left for us to transform, the most sinister angel of all, the Angel of Death, is given permission to take us out.

Death comes when the soul is no longer able to do its job in its current body. The soul must now go to another level. Whether a person leaves this world and moves to the next level as a result of a blessing or because he or she needed a new vehicle (that is, a new body) to do the job is not for anyone to judge. However, no matter what the reason, it is the Angel of Death that takes the soul.

26. THE TEN SEFIROT: THE STRUCTURE OF THE UNIVERSE

We move now from your personal angels to the permanent angels—those infinite beings that rule the universe. In order to understand their place, it's helpful to visualize the underlying structure of the universe.

According to the Zohar, the universe has ten dimensions which are called Sefirot. The word Sefira derives from the Aramaic word for "number" and "communication," so the Sefirot are the means by which we count or measure the universe. They are also the system God uses to communicate with his Creation. If it weren't for the Ten Sefirot, the infinite Creator would be absolutely unknowable and unreachable.

In order from closest to the Light of the Creator to furthest away, the Sefirot are:

Keter: Crown
Chochmah: Divine Wisdom
Binah: Intelligence (Understanding)
Chesed: Mercy and Compassion
Gevurah: Strength and Judgment
Tiferet: Truth (Beauty)

Netzach: Victory (Endurance)
Hod: Majesty (Glory)
Yesod: Foundation
Malchut: Physical

We live in the realm of the tenth Sefira, Malchut, the dimension most material and furthest from the Light of the Creator. This is the physical world, the World of Questions.

Kabbalists teach that as the Light of the Creator moves from Its Source into our world, It passes through this series of veils represented by the Sefirot. Each level filters out some Light until all the Light has been blocked and we arrive at our world of Malchut. The essence of the Light has not changed from one Sefira to the next, but the Light that is revealed diminishes from each level to the next.

Superstring theorists are only now recognizing the uncanny resemblance between these truths of the universe revealed by kabbalists 2000 years ago and their own most advanced explanations of the cosmos. Kabbalah teaches that there are ten dimensions to the universe and so does Superstring theory. Kabbalah also teaches that six of the ten Sefirot are compacted into one dimension, and so do the physicists!

There are four archangels, each of whom governs a specific Sefira. So let's look at them more closely.

27. THE ARCHANGELS

The most illustrious of the permanent angels are the four archangels: Michael, Gabriel, Uriel, and Raphael. According to the Zohar, each archangel presides over one of the four elements and one of the four Sefirot:

Michael, Gabriel, Uriel and Raphael, who are the living creatures of the chariot, control man's four good elements, which are water, fire, wind and earth (which are the secret of the Chesed and Gevurah, Tiferet and Malchut.)

Each archangel is identified with a symbolic animal. Each also governs a color and one of the four directions:

There are four directions in the world—north, south, east, and west—and the archangels guard us in our travels along them. They also administer the flow of energy as it travels from place to place, so one specific angel is given the task of governing each direction.

When you are born, the four archangels accompany you to your new home, and they remain accessible to you as long as the Good Inclination holds sway.

Before all this, four angels descended with him, as is written: "For He shall give His angels charge over you" (Psalms 91:11). If he has ancestral merit, then one is Michael by the merit of Abraham, the second is Gabriel by the merit of Isaac, the third who descends with him is Uriel by the merit of Jacob, and the fourth is Raphael by the merit of Adam. And the Good Inclination is above him.

So let us study each of the four archangels more carefully.

28. THE ARCHANGEL MICHAEL: CLOTHE YOURSELF IN MERCY

Michael, who came to inform Sarah that she shall bear a son, rules over the Right Side. All the abundance and the blessings of the Right Side are handed over to him.

If archangels are the kings of the celestial hierarchy, Michael is the king of kings. His name means "Who is as God." In all traditions, Michael has been recognized as the supreme archangel. He is the angel to call upon when you seek repentance, righteousness, and above all, mercy. We are constantly between two poles in the universe: mercy and judgment—Chesed and Gevurah. Mercy is the force that softens judgment, and Michael is a warrior for that goodness.

Michael stayed the hand of Abraham when he was called to sacrifice his only son, Isaac. And it was Michael who fought the Angel of Death for the body of Moses at his burial. In a portion of the Dead Sea Scrolls entitled "War of the Sons of Light against the Sons of Darkness," Michael is identified as the Prince of Light—a warrior battling valiantly in the cosmic siege against the angels of darkness. He is the winged avenger of righteousness, depicted in paintings with his sword unsheathed, locked in mortal combat with a dragon.

This is a war that has raged throughout history—a battle against Evil itself, embodied by the Angel of Death. This war is still going on, of course, every day, within each of us. And in this war, we need Michael every bit as much as Isaac did.

According to the Zohar, Michael sits to the right side of the Creator, with "water and hail." He is the king of the Right Column, positive energy. He represents the dimension of sharing and blessings.

In this domain, Michael rules over the South and is identified with the color white. White, the color of sharing, represents purity. It does not pull light into itself, but reflects it outward. White light is comprised of all the other colors simultaneously (think of a prism refracting light into a dazzling rainbow). White is the color of the Desire to Share. In the 16th century, Rav Isaac Luria created a tradition among kabbalists that continues to this day: on the Shabbat, men wear white clothing to embody sharing and a diminishment of ego.

Michael is represented by the lion, as we see in the poetic words of the Zohar: "During morning prayer, the lion descends to receive the prayer with its four arms and wings. This is angel Michael."

29. THE ARCHANGEL GABRIEL: THE PRINCE OF JUSTICE

And Gabriel, who came to overturn Sodom, rules over the Left Side and is responsible for all Judgments in the world, as judgments come from the Left Side.

Judgment and Mercy—Gevurah and Chesed—are the twin poles of the universe. Depending on our actions, we move between them. We earn mercy from acts of sharing, but bring judgment upon ourselves when ego runs the show.

Mercy, as we've seen, is the job of Archangel Michael. Judgment is Gabriel's domain. So we can call upon Gabriel when we need to apply judgment in our lives, when we need to define and discern, when we need to make those difficult decisions or calls of justice.

Gabriel's name means "Strength of God." Some sages have placed him at the fifth Sefira, Gevurah. Gevurah represents strength, and we can see a common root in the words: Gevurah and *Gabriel*. Other sages, however, place *Gabriel* lower down, at the ninth Sefira called Yesod, which is just one level above Malchut, our physical reality. According to this view of Gabriel, the archangel uses his strength to support the foundations of the universe.

Archangel Gabriel embodies the dominion of strength over gentleness. He is represented by the ox, which tramples everything in its path. He rules over the North and governs the left side, or Left Column energy, the side of receiving. His color is red, the color of blood. Unlike white, which reflects light away from itself, red has tremendous Desire to Receive; it is self-centered and pulls light in toward itself. It is the color of selfishness. Sometimes we need to receive to be able to share. Gabriel assists us in receiving. Gabriel is a judge.

Whereas Michael sits on the Creator's right, Gabriel, accompanied by two appointed chieftains, the angels Kaftziel and Chezkiel, sits at God's left with fire. Gabriel is the minister of peace between them.

According to the ancient *Talmud*, the Creator instructed Gabriel "Go and write on the forehead of the righteous signs so no sabotage angels can harm them. Go to the evils and write a sign on their forehead so sabotage angels can harm them."

So Gabriel, the judge of us all, writes on our foreheads. He discerns and marks an invisible "R" for righteousness when we curb our self-centered nature and resist reactive behavior. That mark is like a celestial seal of approval; destructive angels take one glance and move on, leaving us in peace. But if we are mired in the Evil Inclination and negativity, Gabriel gives us a different mark. Then, as the ancient texts say, "the sabotage angels" will wreak their justice on us.

The Zohar describes this process in colorful terms: "During the afternoon prayer, the ox descends to receive the prayer with its horns and wings and this is the angel Gabriel." Further on, it says: "His horns ascend from between his two eyes. He observes angrily, and the eyes glow like a burning fire. He rams and tramples with his feet and has no mercy."

There is no mercy when judgment is done. Gabriel engineered the destruction of the sinful cities, Sodom and Gomorrah. In the ancient commentary known as the *Midrash*, he wrought justice on the ten martyred sages. As one of the martyrs ascended to Heaven, he asked Gabriel why they merited death. Gabriel replied that they were restoring the energy that the sin of the ten sons of Jacob who sold Joseph into slavery had removed. He restores the balance by defining the judgment.

A war rages inside each of us between the Evil Inclination and the Good Inclination. Our merits and sins are always wrestling within us. Gabriel represents the Good Inclination, and according to the sages, he wrestles with man before he is born and "teaches him 70 languages." The Evil Inclination then causes man to forget the 70 languages when he is born.

We earn judgments with our negative actions, and according to the Zohar, Gabriel travels with no less than the Evil Angel, handing out judgment to human beings. "Gabriel and the Angel of Death both judge the average person."

But there is a difference. When we transform our Desire to Receive for the Self Alone and move toward the Light and spirituality, Gabriel turns his judgments into blessings.

30. THE ARCHANGEL URIEL: THE FIRE OF GOD

We all want balance in our lives. Central Column energy balances the clash between sharing and receiving, between mercy and judgment. Governing this balancing act is the job of the Archangel Uriel. Uriel is represented by the color green, which according to the Zohar is the color of the Central Column.

In the sacred book of "Enoch," it is written that "Uriel watches over thunder and terror."

The name Uriel means "Fire of God," but the word is derived from the Hebrew word, which means "light." So Uriel can also be called "The Light of God." He is the Great Balancer and a powerful force to bring into your life.

He occupies the middle position on the Ten Sefirot, the Sefira Tiferet, the dimension of Truth. His two celestial traveling companions are the angels Shamsiel and Chasdiel.

Uriel rules over the month of September and the West. He is represented by the eagle, a bird that soars above conflict. When we need to rise above a situation, when we need to restore balance, when we need to take ourselves out of the picture so we can see the true picture, Uriel can help us to see the truth.

31. THE ARCHANGEL RAPHAEL: HEAL THE EARTH

Raphael, who governs the power to heal, helped Abraham.

Kabbalah teaches that disease means "dis-ease," something out of balance. Kabbalah also tells us that nothing happens in the physical realm that doesn't first occur in the metaphysical world. Think of the spiritual world as a computer and the physical world as a printout. The real decisions are made at the software level. Those decisions then manifest physically as a printed document. But if you need to correct the text, you must go back to the computer, fix the error, and then reprint the document.

In the spiritual world, decisions are made at the level of consciousness. Sickness, therefore, arises from that level, too. So to address illness, we must go back to consciousness. One way to do this is to call upon the Archangel Raphael.

Raphael is a special archangel indeed, whose singular job is healer of the earth. Raphael's very name means "God has healed." When affliction strikes, we must clothe ourselves in Raphael's energy. In the Zohar, Rav Abba states that "Raphael is charged to heal the earth and through him, the earth furnishes an abode for man, whom also he heals of his maladies."

Raphael's job description also appears in the sacred book of "Enoch." Raphael is cited as "one of four presences set over all the diseases and all the wounds of the children of men."

Like Uriel, Raphael represents Central Column, or balanced, energy to heal our wounds. His color, too, is green, which is also the color for healing. He governs the direction of the East. Raphael is represented by the face of man, referred to by the Zohar as: "the beast who can speak." He rules over our physical dominion, the realm of manifestation, the World of Questions as the kabbalists have called it—Malchut, the Sefira furthest from the Light.

Raphael was one of three angels who visited Abraham to heal the intense pain of the circumcision Abraham had undergone. And when Jacob wrestled furiously with the angel, it was Raphael who was there to heal the injury to his thigh.

Rav Isaac Luria (the Ari) said: "Raphael is in charge of the desire chamber and this chamber awakens the Malchut." What does this mean?

As you may recall, a Vessel was created in the Endless World to receive the Light that the Creator shared in abundance. That Light is Desire. Without desire, there can be no manifestation of Light. We are all aspects of the Vessel; we are desire incarnate. Desire is the motivating force of the universe, and angels guard the gates of the Realm of Manifestation. We need these angels in order to grow. Only when there is true desire for the Light do the angels allow potential energy to manifest into actual. Raphael rules over desire and can help us to direct our desire to become the true desire—the desire for the Light.

32. RAZI"EL: THE PRIMORDIAL ANGEL

Though not one of the four archangels, this extraordinary being was the first permanent angel. The name Razi"el means "angel of mysteries" or "angel of secrets." In the beginning, Kabbalah teaches that the Light created the Vessel to receive Its beneficence. At that point, all the angels were combined into one force. Razi"el was the Vessel in angelic form. He was all angels. When the Vessel shattered, that one primordial angel exploded into billions of particles, which is why we have innumerable angelic influences today.

Razi"el is the personification of the Sefira Chochmah, which is the seat of Divine Wisdom.

According to sages, the book of the angel Razi"el, known as the *Sefer Razi"el*, was presented to Adam in the Garden of Eden. It was passed from the hand of God, through the medium of the angel Razi"el, to the hand of the first man. The Book of Razi"el is the first book ever written. Certainly, it is the only known book that was actually prepared in Heaven, sent to Earth, and exists in fragments to this day!

Here is what the Zohar says about the *Book of Razi"el*:

> *Observe that the book of the generations of Adam was that which was the Holy One through the angel Razi"el, guardian of the great mysteries and secret doctrine, gave unto Adam while yet in the Garden of Eden. In it was written all the secret wisdom and knowledge concerning the divine name of seventy-two letters and its esoteric six hundred and seventy mysteries. It also contained the fifteen hundred keys, the knowledge and understanding of which had never been imparted to anyone, not even to angels, before it came into possession of Adam.*

With this book, Razi"el became Adam's teacher, initiating him in all orders of knowledge, both celestial and earthly. The Zohar mentions that in the middle of the book is a secret passage explaining the 1500 keys to the mystery of the world, which were not revealed even to the holy angels. But as legend has it, because of Razi"el's privileged status with Adam, the other angels grew envious. Driven by jealousy, they stole the precious book from Adam and tossed it out to sea. God is then said to have commanded Rahab, a primal angel and demon of the deep, to fish out the book and restore it to Adam, which he proceeded to do.

The book, returned to Adam, was then passed through the generations. It educated Noah in its secrets, and through it, Noah learned the art of building an ark. Solomon was next. He is said to have drawn his immense knowledge from the magic in the *Book of Razi"el.*

33. ANGELS OF THE DAY

Each day of the week has a particular energy, so it is governed by a unique angel tasked with providing you support and protection for that day. Angels of the Day are specific packets of energy that control each day.

SUNDAY: From a kabbalistic viewpoint, the first day of the week is Sunday. What is Sunday? Day One of the Universe. It is the day of Creation, the entry point of the Lightforce of the Creator. On this day, we can tap into the seed of everything, the DNA of the universe, and on this day, there are no separations between day and night. There is only Light and blessing.

MONDAY: Why do we get the blues on Monday? There's a good reason. This second day of the week represents the birth of Heaven and Hell—the origin of physicality. Monday is the only day about which God does *not* say: "It is good." The energy of Monday is framed by the birth of chaos, war, disease, and all the other horrors of our physical world since the dawn of time. It's safe to say that from a kabbalistic perspective, Monday is a negative day, and you will need all the assistance from angels you can get. It is a day without blessing. If you are about to embark on an important project, be it a new business or elective surgery, try finding another day. Perhaps Tuesday.

TUESDAY: This is a day of rejuvenation, and according to the Bible, this is the day that grass and trees were created. But Tuesday is not about physicality. The energy of Tuesday is the idea of waters being gathered back together, of that which has been separated being reunited, of the Light and the Vessel returning to their original unity. Judgment is removed on this day. Tuesday is the perfect day for beginnings.

WEDNESDAY: On Wednesday, the sun and the moon were created, and these two luminous beings competed to establish who would rule.

The conflict between the sun and the moon gave birth to what Kabbalah considers perhaps the most dangerous force on Earth: jealousy. Jealousy kills the person who is envied as well as the person who envies, and in the transaction, nothing changes hands but negative energy. Thus, Wednesday symbolizes the birth of Satan as the Negative Force, an insidious Opponent in our lives, who lives inside us and constantly steers our thoughts toward destruction. Not a positive day.

THURSDAY: This is a neutral day with no energy to dramatically call attention to itself. Thursday is more of a bridge day to Friday.

FRIDAY: Friday is the sixth day. It is the day the beasts were created, but more importantly, it is the day man was created. Man was last, indicating his unique nature. But man swings between extremes: He can either be the most important aspect

of Creation, or the least important. The Zohar states that if a man does not evolve, even a mosquito is more spiritually advanced than he is. A mosquito does its job with singular focus. It drinks blood. Man, on the other hand, is touched by a strange madness. What other creature kills for fun? Still, man is also the only creature who can evolve and transform his nature. That is our job, at least when our consciousness is high enough to recognize it.

In General, Friday is a positive day, as we begin the transition into Shabbat. At the noon hour there is a fight between the negative energy forces of the week and the positive energy of Shabbat. We say *kegavna*, as a way to protect us from the negative angels that depart before we enter Shabbat.

SATURDAY: Shabbat is so holy that it's not considered a day, but rather a special window of connection to the World of Answers. On this day, the Light is given freely to humans simply by virtue of the day.

34. THE ANGELS OF THE ZODIAC

Just as there are angels for each day of the week, there are also angels governing each of the twelve signs of the Zodiac. The *Sefer Yetzirah* (Book of Formation) explained the laws of astrology, and since that time, both the power of the planets and signs of the Zodiac have been keys to kabbalistic knowledge. The following esoteric passage reveals the link between angels and the signs:

> *And the 12 triangle borders (that surrounding Sefira Yesod, 12 tribes, 12 months of the year, different directions), they have also Emanated angels, because their name will indicate their army... and an evidence for that is the result of a world, a year, a soul, we interpreted that there are 12 signs in the world and few forces in each sign and in the months of the year and so in the organs.*

Our *tikkun*, or correction, is intimately bound up with our astrological chart since each sign represents a specific challenge we need to overcome. We can also ask for angelic assistance in the month represented by the zodiac sign each angel embodies.

Aries: You were born under a cardinal fire sign and are challenged by issues of ego and self-centeredness. Aries is ruled

by the angel Uriel. Ask him for help in recognizing others' needs and opening to them. This is the growth for an Aries.

Taurus: You were born under a fixed earth sign, and as the words "fixed earth" imply, you are challenged by laziness, stubbornness, and an unwillingness to venture from the comfort zone. Taurus is governed by the angel Lahati"el. Ask him for help in freeing you from limiting safety of routine.

Gemini: You were born under a mutable air sign. You tend to be likeable but have trouble sticking with projects and following through. Gemini is supervised by the angel Pni"el. Ask him to help you finish what you start.

Cancer: You were born under a cardinal water sign and are challenged by extreme sensitivity. Cancer is ruled by the angel Zuri"el. Ask him for help in freeing yourself from over-sensitivity and the tendency to dwell on the past so you can move on and complete your *tikkun*.

Leo: You were born under a fixed fire sign. You have great leadership abilities but an inclination to talk too much. Leo is governed by the angel Barki"el. Ask him for help in giving others a chance and opening yourself to learn from them.

Virgo: You were born under a mutable earth sign. You have great energy for service but a tendency to be nitpicky and critical. Virgo is ruled by the angel Chani"el. Ask him for help in

overcoming the need to correct and control others, and for help in letting go, a prime requirement for growth.

Libra: You were born under a cardinal air sign. You have a quality of balance that is sometimes an obstacle to making a decision. Libra is governed by the angel Tzuri"el. Ask him for help in committing to a path that will help you transcend your nature and grow.

Scorpio: You were born under a fixed water sign and are challenged by issues of power and control. Scorpio is ruled by the angel Gabriel. Ask him for help in releasing the need to control others.

Sagittarius: You were born under a mutable fire sign, with great energy but challenges when it comes to commitment. Sagittarius is governed by the angel Me'adoni"el. Ask him for help in staying the course and seeing it through.

Capricorn: You were born under a cardinal earth sign, with a capacity for hard work but challenges of unhappiness. Capricorn is ruled by the angel Shni"el. Ask him for help in rising beyond the confines of physicality and realizing the spiritual nature of the universe.

Aquarius: You were born under a fixed air sign. You have great idealism but a need to rebel and be free from most things. Aquarius is governed by the angel Gabriel. Ask him for help in

understanding the physical world and the requirements for living in it as you complete your correction.

Pisces: You were born under a mutable water sign, with great sensitivity but challenges when it comes to being firm and definite. Pisces is ruled by the angel Rumi"el. Ask him for help in overcoming your overly sensitive nature and in gaining clarity on what you need in life.

35. ANGELS FOR OUR CHILDREN

According to an ancient text called *Sefer Hatmuna*, the angel Sandalfon watches over fetuses in the wombs of each and every pregnant woman. He determines the child's gender.

> *The angel Sandalfon gives print and a drop inside the womb, who will be male and who will be female. He keeps the drop until it goes outside.*

The angel Layl"ah (Whose name we don't pronounce) has the important role of overseeing the birth of the children as well as their destiny. Layl"ah proclaims whether new babies will be strong or weak, wise or foolish, rich or poor. And as they grow, the *Sefer Hatmuna* explains that another angel, Pani"el, is charged with the wonderful task of tending to their happiness and spirituality.

> *...those merciful angels never change and continue doing one mission. And they cannot be seen unless someone is very happy. In charge of this chamber is Paniel.*

36. THE ANGELS OF HAPPINESS

Kabbalah teaches that true happiness isn't a reaction to external events. You may have finally bought the car you were longing for, got that raise you'd hoped for, or met the girl of your dreams, but before long, that euphoria dissipates.

Joy does not arise in response to external stimuli. In fact, the energy of bliss works in the opposite way. Happiness is a force that emanates from within us. When we bring our happiness to the world, the most ordinary experiences—a burnished leaf, the sky at dawn, a friendly smile, the sound of rain on the roof, a crackling fire—evoke delight. Suddenly, these experiences are no longer mundane. *This* is the nature of true appreciation.

Joy overwhelms the senses and conquers the world of questions, opening up the gates of Light. The energy of angels is the seed of such true happiness. Indeed, we can summon the angels of happiness and make them manifest by uttering a single Aramaic word: *Chidu*. In Part III, I'll tell you more specifically how to do this.

37. METATR"ON: FROM HUMAN TO ANGELIC

The angel Metatr"on (Whose name we don't pronounce) is unique in all the celestial hierarchy because he is the only angel who began life in human form but through spiritual work and transformation ascended to angelic status. As a man, he was known as Enoch. When God transformed him into an angel, he was awarded the name Metatr"on.

The Zohar identifies Metatr"on as the angel who led the people of Israel through the wilderness after their exodus from Egypt. But having come from human origin, by virtue of this enormous accomplishment, he now rules higher than any angel.

Metatr"on transmits the daily orders of God to the Archangel Gabriel as well as to the Angel of Death. And this brings us to the second type of permanent angels—those whom you do not wish to draw down upon yourself because they rule over the Evil Inclination.

38. NEGATIVE ANGELS

The Zohar describes the demons of the world, the "angels of destruction," in the following way:

> *And there are natural living creatures, namely angels appointed over bodies that are of the four basic elements: fire, wind, water, and earth, and they are pure. Opposed to them are four living creatures of prey, namely the angels of destruction.*

We do not speak the names of the dark angels for fear of drawing them to our side. But we do encounter them, especially at times of calamity. When the World of Answers collides with the World of Questions, when the spiritual meets the physical, there is a violent flash of connection. Tremors split the Earth, and we call the result earthquakes.

Geologists consider these convulsions to be random and unpredictable, resulting from great plates shifting deep below the Earth's surface. But the Zohar explains that the devastation, like all else on the physical plane, has its cause in the spiritual world. Consciousness is the creator of physical events, so when terrible calamities arise, they have been evoked by our collective consciousness. And an earthquake means that the angels of destruction are taking over.

Rav Yitzchak came upon a mountain and saw a man sleeping under a tree. Rav Yitzchak sat down there. While he was sitting, he noticed the Earth moving and saw that tree break and fall. He saw fissure holes in the Earth, and the Earth was rising and falling.

The man awoke and screamed towards Rav Yitzchak: "Cry and wail because now they are setting up in heaven a minister, a supernal ruler, who is destined to do great evil with your people. These tremors in the Earth are because of you, for whenever the Earth rumbles, it is when a minister arises in the heaven who will do evil with you!"

Sama"el (whose name we do not pronounce) is the code name for the supreme trickster. Master and commander of negative angels, he constantly urges us toward evil. He never tells exactly what to do. No, the commander just puts the inclination in our heads.

Sama"el lives, according to the Zohar, in the Milky Way, in league with his satanic army. And it is interesting to note that recently, science discovered a monster black hole in the Milky Way galaxy.

The name Sama"el is derived from the word *sami*, which means "blind." The suffix -el which means God. *Blind of God*. He is linked to Mars, the planet of war, and connected to the Sefira Gevurah, which denotes judgment and power. Kabbalists have

been divided about Sama"el throughout history, some placing him at the head of a demonic hierarchy alongside his wife Lili"th (whose name we also do not pronounce or call out loud, for doing so brings her chaos into our lives), while others have viewed him simply as an unpleasant but necessary component of Creation.

39. A ROGUES' GALLERY

Sages have estimated there are thousands upon thousands of angels of destruction. What can Satan's mischievous minions do? To start with, they might keep you on the streets on Wednesday and Friday nights. Yes, it is written in the ancient texts that you must be extremely wary of going out alone on those nights because these are times when a supremely negative angel, Iger"et Bat Macha"la, sows mischief, and he does so in league with 180,000 sabotaging angels, each of whom can cause damage to human beings.

Seven of these negative angels have come to be known as the Angels of Confusion. God dispatched them to the court of King Ahashverosh in the time of Queen Esther to punish and confound the king. These angels may also have been present at the Tower of Babel—when a multiplicity of languages was born and confusion was thrust permanently upon mankind—to sow chaos on earth.

Seven angels also rule over Hell. They are presided over by Dumah. His nefarious followers in the sinister celestial realm include Kushi"el, Lahati"el, Shafti"el, Machti"el, Chutri"el, and Pusi"el. There are also angels involved in tricks and opposition. They block our way and hinder our progress. In fact, two of

them, Aza and Aza"el, opposed the creation of man from the beginning:

> *When the Shechinah said to the Holy One, blessed be He, "Let us make man," Aza and Aza"el responded, "What is man that you take knowledge of him?" (Psalms 144:3). "Why do You wish to create man when You know that he shall definitely sin before you, with his wife."*

40. THE ANGELS OF DEATH

More than a dozen angels of death have been mentioned in spiritual writings over the course of time. Some have been assigned specific jobs:

- Gabriel rules over the death of young people.
- Mash"hit oversees the death of children.
- Kafzi"el watches over the death of kings.
- Meshabb"er and Hem"ah have dominion over animals.

However, Satan is the ultimate Angel of Death. It is written in ancient texts that Satan doesn't stop at the grave. If his victim has not grown spiritually during life, if the Desire to Receive for the Self Alone persists, Satan sends a horrifying army of avenging angels who beat the body even in its resting site.

This raises an interesting question. If one is already dead, would this beating matter? Would one even feel it? But Kabbalah teaches that we have consciousness even in death. Indeed, our consciousness is determined by which one of the three levels of soul we inhabit.

The lowest is known in Aramaic as Nefesh, and it is closest to an animal soul. If you live brutishly, this is where your consciousness

will reside, and you will continue to suffer even in the grave. But if you've worked on yourself spiritually, achieving transformation and some degree of spiritual elevation, you attain Ruach, the next level of consciousness. Then, once you die, you are not truly in your grave, but somewhere between Heaven and Earth. And those who reach Neshamah, the highest level, don't experience death at all.

But remember, the Angel of Death represents not just physical demise, but a death energy that spreads to our relationships, our businesses, and our dreams. He is the embodiment of the Evil Inclination—a trickster with two sides, male and female. When he plays to us, we are charmed by his wiles; a lie is spun with a tiny grain of truth at its center, and the Angel of Death gains entry through the back door.

During our lives, the Angel of Death feasts on our negativity and ego, our Desire to Receive for the Self Alone. Our anger, hatred, and greed provide energy to the Angel of Death every day.

Heart attack, cancer, stroke, car accident, or suicide? The cause of death listed in the medical examiner's report is never the real reason of our demise—it is only the effect. When we die, it is because the Angel of Death was given permission to end the game due to our karma, our actions.

41. THE ANGELS OF THE CHAMBERS OF THE UNIVERSE

The architecture of the spiritual world is vaster and more mysterious than we can possibly imagine. I've described the ten Sefirot, but there are also the five separate worlds of the universe as depicted in Jacob's ladder, the three levels of soul that I alluded to earlier, and the seven spiritual "chambers" in the world of Creation. Every human soul inhabits one of these chambers according to his or her merit, and each chamber has an angel who guards and governs it.

The First or highest Chamber is the ultimate. Here the souls of the righteous bask in what the holy books call "peace, blessings and treasures." The angel Adrahni"el is in charge here.

The Second Chamber is the world quite close to the Kingdom of Heaven. The angel in charge here is Ori"el. Living in the rarefied realm of this Second Chamber is a special group of souls: the spirits of those who were unjustly killed by humans and whose deaths deserve to be avenged. This portion of the chamber is governed by the angel Adarni'el.

Angels of mercy live in the Third Chamber. Kadshi"el is the angel in charge here. Part of the Third Chamber is reserved for the souls of those who were taken to Hell because they wanted to repent on Earth but didn't manage to finish the job by the time

they died. When they have completed their course of healing in Hell, the angel Adrahni"el brings them up again, and they live in relative tranquility in this, the Third Chamber.

The Fourth Chamber contains the Supreme Angels of the Right Column, the Column of sharing and positive energy. The souls of the people who reside in this chamber no longer die and get reborn. Having attained their correction, they just exist here. Governing this chamber is the angel Pada"el.

In the Fifth Chamber live the Sabotaging Angels of the Left Column. The Left Column represents the Desire to Receive for the Self Alone, the energy of ego, negativity, and disconnection from the Light. This is the dwelling place of those who did not correct themselves while in their body. A portion of this chamber is reserved for what are called "foreigner's souls," and this portion is ruled by the angel Sama"el (Whose name we don't pronounce).

The only positive thing that can be said about the Sixth Chamber is that it is not as dark as the Seventh. But here, in the second to last chamber, it is very dark indeed. Some light penetrates, however, for the angels in the Sixth Chamber encourage people to study and work with the Zohar, which is a spiritual power source. The angel in charge of this realm is Kdumi"el.

Finally, we come to the lowest chamber, the one most removed from the Endless World and the Light. Sages describe "ghost spirits without form and shape wandering at night" in its bleak landscape. The angel in charge of the dark realm of the Seventh Chamber is Tahari"el.

42. THE ANGELS OF JUDGMENT

How is it determined which souls are righteous and which continue to need correction, which ones rest in the First Chamber of the universe, and which are relegated to the Seventh? Again, this is the role of angels. As we live out our individual destinies, a team of angels watches over us and delivers a verdict on our actions.

> At the first gate stands the chief Malki"el, in charge over the notes on which the verdict is written, emerging from the King's court that judges the world. This chief supervises over these notes, with two scribes under him, one to the right and one to the left.
>
> Malki"el is given the notes to be corrected, before they leave the gate, to be handed to the chieftain of the first chamber. Once they are given to the chieftain of the first chamber, they leave the place, and there is no possibility to return them so as to correct them.

According to ancient texts, angels oversee the scales, weighing our sins against our merits. They are our judges as we labor in what is called the "gruesome mud" of the Evil Inclination, doing our best to get out of "debt."

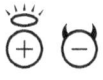

> *As for all the precepts in the world, the holy angels, appointed over the merits in the world, take them and put them in the fourth chamber OF HOLINESS called 'merit', where the precepts of men abide. And the sins are in the other chamber called 'debt'. They are balanced on Rosh Hashana, for "the Elohim has made the one as well as the other" (Kohelet 7:14), and according to the tipping of the scales by the precepts or sins, this or that side wins. IF THERE ARE MORE SINS, THE OTHER SIDE WINS, AND IF THERE ARE MORE PRECEPTS, THE HOLINESS WINS.*

Other angels watch over the well-intentioned. These are the people with a strong desire to do spiritual work. They think positive thoughts and perform good actions, but they are simply unable to raise themselves to a higher consciousness. According to ancient texts, these striving souls are not forgotten. They have unique angels who protect them:

> *An angel also rules those who need repentance but who have not transformed their natures sufficiently. Unfortunately, they merit effects of their actions because they have not changed their consciousness sufficiently to transform the effects to blessings.*

Of course, none of us wish to find ourselves so judged. But through repentance, prayer, good deeds, and charity, which in Aramaic is called *tzadaka* we have the ability to transform ourselves.

Part III

Send Me an Angel

You now have a good sense of the roster of players—those permanent angels that are important aspects of the consciousness and actions in your life.

Angels can be seen directly, and certainly there are people who see them. Some may even hear them. But seeing angels isn't really the point. Calling them to our side is the key to using angels in our lives. In the following pages, I will show you how.

43. THE TECHNOLOGY OF THE SOUL

Knowledge of angels gives us access to a set of tools that can help us enjoy lives free of chaos. The greater our awareness, the more positive angels we will draw to help guide us. This book is a tool to build that awareness and that army of positive angels on the right. But how do we do that?

Think about how we use our computers. We don't need to understand the workings of our circuit boards to send an email, do we? No, all we have to do is click on the SEND icon and our electronic missive whisks into cyberspace.

Angels are a technology, just like our computers. Our good behaviors click on helpful email messages, trigger the SEND key, and positive angels show up in our lives. We initiate the action and the angels move into place, providing support and follow-through.

In addition to these temporary angels, there will always be times when we need to use a specific permanent angel.

Kabbalah provides a means to gain access to the invisible network of angels so we can unlock and harness their power. In fact, Kabbalah is a vast directory of angels, listing the job they do and the domain they govern. How do we call them? We pray.

44. CONNECTING TO YOUR ANGELS

Angels are our ticket—our transportation system—allowing movement between the World of Questions and the World of Answers. How do we connect with angels?

Through prayer.

For kabbalists, prayer is nothing less than a means to participate in the quantum dynamics of the universe.

"Quantum" is a scholarly, scientific word, but its meaning is simple and amazing: in ways we cannot perceive, everything in the universe is connected and everything affects everything else. While normal consciousness perceives separation and disconnection, ancient sages and leading-edge scientists both teach of a higher reality and a more fundamental unity.

Brian Greene, professor of physics and mathematics at Columbia University, describes quantum dynamics this way:

> *Quantum mechanics challenges this [conventional] view of space by revealing, at least in certain circumstances, a capacity to transcend space; long-range quantum connections can bypass spatial separation. Two objects can be far apart in space, but*

as far as quantum mechanics is concerned, it's as if they're a single entity.

Prayer is a way to access this connection and to restore this primordial unity between all things. Through prayer and connecting to the angels, positive changes will come into your life, even though the mechanism for these changes is invisible.

However, your prayer cannot be merely empty thoughts or words. According to the Zohar:

> *Prayer is made up of both action and speech, and when the action is faulty, speech does not find a spot to rest in; such prayer is not prayer, and the man offering it is defective in the Upper and the Lower Worlds.*

The Zohar teaches us that to be effective, prayer must be accompanied by action. The term for this is *kavanah*, or directed attention and concentration surrounding the words of a prayer. The great 11th century Kabbalist, Rav Bachye Ibn Paquda, even stated that prayer without *kavanah* is like a body without a soul or a husk without a kernel. The words of a prayer are the channel for the more important aspect of *kavanah*, which is the soul of the prayer.

Your destiny is a function of your consciousness. It is not enough to go through the motions of praying. Your level of consciousness

and true actions will determine whether you connect to the Higher Realms and are able to erase the negative energy that has accumulated around you. That means your prayer can't be routine or rote. "He that makes his prayer a fixed task," warned Rav Eliezer, "his prayer is not a prayer."

A band of angels accepts or rejects prayers, depending on the level of purity of the person doing the praying. Rejected or unfit prayers are not destroyed; they are stored and re-submitted to God when the person repents. Here's how the Zohar describes it.

> *If the prayer is solitary, it rises until it reaches the entrance of this chamber, where the chieftain stands. If it is good enough to be presented before the Holy King, he immediately opens the door and lets it in. If it is not worthy, he pushes it out, and it goes down and hovers about the world, standing at the lowest of the firmaments in the world below, where there is a chieftain by the name of Sahadi'el, in charge over that firmament. He takes all the rejected prayers, called 'unfit prayers,' and stores them until that person transforms.*
>
> *If he properly repents before his Master, and prays another, good prayer, then when the good one rises, the chieftain Sahadi'el take the UNFIT prayer and elevates it, until it meets the good prayer and they both rise and intermingle and come before the Holy King.*

The Aramaic word for prayer, *tefillah*, actually can be translated as "secondary," or even "trivial." But this does not mean the words of the prayer are unnecessary. The soul needs a body to express itself within physical existence, and consciousness needs the words and letters of our prayers to manifest itself within the physical domain.

When we complete prayer in the kabbalistic sense, we instill the ever-present Light in our awareness. It is beyond our perception to understand how this works, but prayer with *kavanah* hotwires us directly to the angels and the Light of the Creator.

Earning the protection of an angel is not an intellectual exercise. Consciousness is the key. Consider the famous kabbalistic spiritual tool known as the Red String. It has a physical form but also a consciousness. This red thread of wool is imbued with the energy of protection of the tomb of Rachel in Israel. We wear the Red String on our left wrist because, according to the Three Column System, the left is the side of receiving. The Red String is designed to protect us from Evil Eye vibrations from the jealousy and envy of other people that bombard us and infiltrate us through our left side. The Red String is a physical object, but it operates in the space where consciousness attaches to the physical.

This space is the domain of the angels. When we wear the Red String, it is the angels who are providing the protection, operating on a spiritual level rather than simply through the

physicality of the Red String. By wearing the Red String, we take on a physical energy that creates miracles.

45. THE LETTERS OF THE ANGELS

So how exactly do you contact angels? And what language do you use to pray to them?

Kabbalah and ancient sacred texts give us a clear sign. In the Book of Formation, Abraham discloses the secret structures of the universe, and one of the keys is the Aramaic language. According to Abraham and all subsequent kabbalists, Aramaic has a unique power. It is not simply a language: Its letters are the alphabet of creation, the DNA of the universe.

Biologists know that all living things are built of four letters: A, T, C and G. These are the genetic alphabet of our DNA. They represent chemicals that combine and create the instructions necessary to build the proteins that support life. Similarly, according to Kabbalah, the universe is built from a genetic alphabet consisting of 22 Aramaic letters. (Aramaic letters and Hebrew letters are the same.) Each of these letters represents a particular energy that combines in specific sequences to build our universe.

Through our prayers and blessings, we can tap into the power of the Aramaic letters, the engines of creation to connect to the Lightforce of God. And we can use Aramaic letters to connect to the angels. Ancient text says, the Aramaic letters are the letters that "God used at Creation and in the Garden of Eden."

But before you throw up your hands and say, "I don't read Aramaic," you need to understand some crucial information about Aramaic and connecting to angels.

Aramaic letters are channels of energy. With the right consciousness, you can connect to this energy simply by scanning these letters, that is, by gazing at particular letter sequences. Passing your eyes over these sequences functions like a scanner at the supermarket. The data goes directly to a computer somewhere. You have no idea where the computer is, but it doesn't matter. The same is true when you scan the names of the angels.

The actual shape and form of the Aramaic letters are designed to channel the creative force of Light into our world and our lives. Your soul can read these letters—*even* if you are illiterate in Aramaic. Put another way: You don't need to understand the code that your computer software is written in. You simply need to know how to power up and start typing. Using Aramaic, the letters of the angels, means simply scanning letters and saying prayers with the proper consciousness.

These sequences have been derived over the millennia through divine inspiration by ancient sages and kabbalists. When you scan them, you are connecting to the invisible energies of a universe beyond your rational mind.

46. HOW TO CONNECT TO THE VOICE OF YOUR GUARDIAN ANGEL

When we're quiet enough, each of us has heard a voice inside, telling us the right path to take. We may not listen, we may push the voice away because we may not want to hear what it has to say—but that would be a mistake. Because this is the voice of our higher self and our Guardian Angel. He has been with us since birth, and he is our connection to the Light.

But how do you quiet yourself enough to gain access to that voice, to hear what guidance your Guardian Angel has to offer you? The following exercise will help. You might want to tape it and play it back to yourself so you don't have to read it. This should take you 15 to 30 minutes.

- Find a positive place where you feel safe and relaxed.
- Light a candle.
- Turn off the lights. Turn off the phone, and make sure you're not disturbed.
- Place your feet flat on the floor and rest your hands on your legs. You should be relaxed. Make sure not to cross your arms or legs.
- Watch the flickering light of the candle.
- Take a few deep breaths.

- Feel the top of your head relaxing, down to your neck, your arms, shoulders, down to the tips of your fingers. You are filled with warmth down your torso, down the spinal column. Fill your chest with Light energy. Deeper, deeper, fill the torso. Now let this energy pour into your thighs, your knees, down the length of the legs, into your feet.
- Surround yourself with a wonderful feeling from the Lightforce seeping into your body, the white light throughout your body, deeper and deeper.
- Now close your eyes. In your mind's eye, walk into a tunnel or walkway, at the end of which there is warm sunlight.
- As you move towards that sunlight, you'll see a door.
- Raise the door as if it were a garage door that opens slowly.
- As you start to raise the door, you will see some form of energy. Don't have any preconceived ideas about what you will see.
- Raise the door a little further. The energy doesn't have to have six white wings. It will take a shape of some kind, but it doesn't have to be a person. Raise the door and let the energy penetrate your thoughts.
- Try to relate to that energy. See if you can create a rapport with it. Go further, go deeper into it. What color is it? Where is it from? Is it warm? What would you like to do with it?

- Know that your Guardian Angel is there for you all the time. All you have to do is ask from within yourself, and your Guardian Angel will make his or her presence known to you.
- Feel your Guardian Angel's warmth and caring. Bask in the Light.
- Now it's time to go back. Just know that this door is here for you to open whenever you need help. If you concentrate and your thoughts are pure, you can go into this meditative state to find it.
- Now imagine yourself looking out onto a spectacular spring day. Look out towards the sun and the beautiful sky, enjoying the smell of the flowers and the warmth of the sun.
- Now count backwards, beginning with ten.
- Take a very deep breath and slowly open your eyes.
- Put the lights on low at first, so your eyes can comfortably acclimate to them.

Try this meditation once or twice a week. Drawing open that door and lifting it in your mind's eye is the most difficult part of this exercise. You're removing negativity, which blocks out the Light. When we have more Light in our lives and more empathy for others, we can reach another stage, another spiritual level.

47. CALLING UPON THE ARCHANGELS

How do you call upon the archangels: Michael, Gabriel, Uriel, and Raphael? It is not simply by calling their names that you invoke their power. Kabbalists teach that you have to clothe yourself in their energy as you call out to them.

For instance, if you want the protection of Michael, you need to clothe yourself, your consciousness, in his energy by performing acts of sharing. Intention and action are all-important. You meditate upon Michael and his name, making a spiritual connection while you share with people—meaning, you take a physical action. In this way, you ignite the qualities of Michael in yourself and in others—the qualities of mercy—and that will lead to the erasure of judgments.

When you clothe yourself in the energy of Gabriel, you embody justice and strength. When you clothe yourself in the energy of Uriel, you balance yourself and, like an eagle, rise above the struggle of the moment. When you clothe yourself in the energy of Raphael, your intention is focused on healing and desire.

48. HOW TO CONTACT THE ANGELS OF THE DAY

Kabbalists have constructed a tool for contacting the Angels of the Day. This is much like a phone directory, although it probably won't resemble any Yellow Pages you know. In fact, this directory is not meant to be read aloud. These are phone numbers you call simply by looking at them.

Each of these seven angels represents the unique energy of its day. If today is Tuesday, open this book to the page for Tuesday's angel and scan the Hebrew letters on the page. It's that simple. Do the same on Wednesday for Wednesday's angel, and Thursday, and so on. The morning is a good time for this practice because there is less clutter in your mind and you'll experience less resistance in connecting to the angel of the day.

But remember, unlike English, Aramaic reads from right to left. So using your finger, slowly scan the letters from right to left one line at a time, from the top of the page to bottom. As you scan, think of the angel of the day sending you energy, offering you protection, empowering you to control the day ahead.

Then sit quietly for a moment. Your eyes can be open or closed, whichever helps you into a deeper, more centered place. This is where you experience what scientists call the alpha state.

Scan the angel of the day every day for two weeks and you will see a difference in the quality of your day.

THE ANGELS OF THE DAY

יום א׳ יֱהֹוִה

SUNDAY

יוֹד הֵי וָו הֵי יֵוֵד הֵי וֵאו הֵי
אל שׁדי יאולדפההייואוודההיי
אנא בכוח גדולת ימינך תתיר צרורה
אבגיתץ יְהֹוֶה יֱהֹוִה
סמטוריה גוריאל וענאל למואל

ר״ת סגול

Angel Intelligence

THE ANGELS OF THE DAY

יוֹם בּ׳

MONDAY

יוֹד הֵי וָאו הֵי וָאו הֵי יוֹד הֵי וָאו הֵי הֵי יוֹד הֵא וָאו הֵא
אל יהוה יאולדפההאאויאוודההאא
קבל רנת עמך שגבנו טהרנו נורא
קְרַעְשְׂטָן יְהֹוָה יְהֹוָה
שְׁמְעִיאֵל בְּרְכִיאֵל אַהֲנִיאֵל

ר"ת שׂוא

Scanning Direction

THE ANGELS OF THE DAY

יוֹם גּ

TUESDAY

יוֹד הֵא וָאו הֵא יוֹד הֵה וָו הֵה
אל אדני יאולדפההההויודההה
נא גבור דורשי יחודך כבבת שמרם
נַגְדִיכַשׁ יֲהֱוַה יהוה
וזניאל להדיאל מוזניאל

ר"ת וזלם

Angel Intelligence

THE ANGELS OF THE DAY

יוֹם ד׳

WEDNESDAY

יוֹד הֹא וֹאוֹ הֹא יוֹד הֵה וָו הֵה
אֵל אֲדֹנָי יאולדפהההוודההתה
בּרכּם טֹהרם רוֹמי צדקתך תמיד גמלם
בַּטַרְצְתַג יֲהֲוָה יְהֹוָה
וֹחֲזקִיאֵל רהטיאֵל קדשׁיאֵל

ר״ת וורק

Scanning Direction

THE ANGELS OF THE DAY

יוֹם הָ

THURSDAY

יוֹד הֵי וָאו הֵי יוֹד הִי וָאו הִי יוֹד הֵא וָאו הֵא
אל יהוה יאולדפההאאיאוודההאא
חֹסִין קָדִישׁ בְּרוֹב טוּבְךָ נַהֵל עֲדָתֶךָ
וַהֲקַבְּטְנַע יֲהֶוַה יֲהֶוַה
שְׁמוּעָאֵל רְעַמִיאֵל קְנִיאֵל

ר"ת שׁעֹרְקָ
(הקיבוץ מלאכיו בר"ת שׁוּעֹרְקָ)

Angel Intelligence

THE ANGELS OF THE DAY

יום ו׳

FRIDAY

יוּד הֵי וֵו הֵי יֶוֶד הֵי וָאו הֵי
אל שׁדי יאולדפההייאודההיי
יוזיד גאה לעמך פנה זוכרי קדושתך
יִגְלְפְזָק יֱהֶוָה יוּהוּווּהוּ
שׁוּמוּשִׁיוִאוֹלוּ רוֹפוֹאוֹלוּ קוּדוֹשִׁיוִאוֹלוּ

ר"ת שׂרק

THE ANGELS OF THE DAY

לֵיל שַׁבָּת

FRIDAY
SHABBAT EVENING

יוֹד הֵי וָאו הֵי

שׁוּעָתֵנוּ קַבֵּל וּשְׁמַע צַעֲקָתֵנוּ יוֹדֵעַ תַּעֲלוּמוֹת

שַׁקוֹצִית יֲהֵוָה יֶהֱוָה יְהֹוָה

שְׁמְעִיאֵל בְּרָכִיאֵל אָהֳנִיאֵל

ר"ת שׁוא

סְמַטוּרְיָה גְּזַרִיאֵל וְעָנָאֵל לָמוּאֵל

ר"ת סגול

צוּרִיאֵל רָזִיאֵל יוֹפִיאֵל

ר"ת צִירִי

Shabbat has additional energy, so we have three separate angel connections.

Angel Intelligence

THE ANGELS OF THE DAY

יוֹם שַׁבָּת

SATURDAY
SHABBAT MORNING

יָוָד הָי וָיו הָי יַוד הַי וַו הַי

שׁוֹעָתֵנוּ קַבֵּל וּשְׁמַע צַעֲקָתֵנוּ יוֹדֵעַ תַּעֲלוּמוֹת

שַׁקְוֻצִית יֲהֶוָה יְהֹוָה יָהָוָה

שְׁמִעְיאֵל בְּרְכִיאֵל אֲהָנִיאֵל

ר"ת שׁוֹא

קַדְמִיאֵל מַלְכִּיאֵל צוּרִיאֵל

ר"ת קִמָ"ץ

← Scanning Direction

THE ANGELS OF THE DAY

מִנְחוֹת שַׁבָּת

SATURDAY
SHABBAT AFTERNOON

יוֹד הֵא וָאו הֵא יוֹד הֵא וָאו הֵא

שׁוַעְתֵּנוּ קַבֵּל וּשְׁמַע צַעֲקָתֵנוּ יוֹדֵעַ תַּעֲלוּמוֹת

שַׁקְוּצִית יְהֹוָה יְהֹוָה יַהֹוַה

שְׁמִעִיאֵל בְּרַכִיאֵל אַהֲנִיאֵל

ר"ת שׁוא

פַּדְאֵל תַּלְמִיאֵל (תּוּמִיאֵל) וְחַסְדִיאֵל

ר"ת פַּתוַח

49. HOW TO CONTACT THE ANGELS OF HAPPINESS

We can summon the angels of happiness and make them manifest by uttering the Aramaic letters Chet, Yud, Dalet, Vav, pronounced *Chidu*. By simply repeating this word aloud, we bring an enormous number of angels into our lives, where they can bring blessings and protection.

When you say the word *Chidu* you draw down gleaming energy from a touchable realm of angels. The name is a tool, and the tool is available for us to use whenever we please—for love, Light, laughter, and healing.

The energy of this word is powerful and profound, connecting directly to the highest circles of Light. We can see Light flowing in those four Aramaic letters: וֹדִיחַ They flood us with the Lightforce that emanates from God and our gleaming universe.

The best way to call the angels of happiness is to find a quiet place where you won't be self-conscious. Then say *Chidu* out loud. Each letter makes a connection for you, tapping into the Lightforce. This direct connection with angels conquers time, space, and the forces of gravity. According to legend, some kabbalists were able to elevate themselves five inches from the ground with the simple repetition of this word.

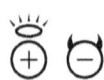

This is the power of laughter and happiness. This is the energy that science concludes can bring healing. When we're happy, we can soar. The day seems to unfold effortlessly. The constant struggle to acquire, to hold, to make things go our way, suddenly seems unnecessary. When the angels support us, when the connection to Light is made, everything that we need starts to show up in our lives as if by magic, just at the precise moment that we need it.

50. THE ANA BEKO'ACH: THE PRAYER OF THE KABBALIST

The Ana Beko'ach (pronounced AH-Na Bi-KO-ach) prayer, or "The Prayer of the Kabbalist," is the most powerful prayer in the universe—a virtual satellite hook-up to a vast array of angels. This is a sequence of Aramaic letters that taps the primordial powers of Creation. Sometimes the prayer is known as "the 42-Letter Name of God" because it contains seven lines of six words each, for a total of 42 words. But most often, it goes by the name of its first two words—Ana Beko'ach.

The 42 words of this prayer give us the ability to connect to the planetary and zodiac signs; in addition, each month has its corresponding verse in the Ana Beko'ach. Its words also enable us to connect to the positive energy of each day, wrapping our lives in healing energy and a shield of protection.

The seven sentences correspond to the seven days of the week. While we recite the entire prayer aloud each day (I recommend twice a day, if possible), we meditate specifically on the sentence associated with the day of the week in which we find ourselves to empower our day with that energy. The first sentence connects us to Sunday, the second to Monday, and so on until the final line connects to Saturday, or Shabbat.

Angel Intelligence

THE ANA BEKO'ACH

❶ חסד, יום ראשון Sunday, Chesed   אבג יתץ

אָ֢נָּ֣א בְּכֹ֖חַ. גְּ֚דוּלַּ֣ת יְמִינְ֒ךָ. תַּתִּ֖יר צְרוּרָֽה:

ana   beko'ach   gedulat   yeminecha   tatir   tzerura

Meditation: Power of redemption. Unconditional love. Removing the negative influence of physical matter from our lives. Tapping into the Tree of Life reality. Remembering yesterdayís lessons.

❷ גבורה, יום שני Monday, Gvurah   קרע שטן

קַבֵּ֣ל רִנַּ֤ת. עַמְּ֨ךָ. שַׂגְּבֵ֑נוּ. טַהֲרֵ֖נוּ נוֹרָֽא:

kabel   rinat   amecha   sagvenu   taharenu   nora

Meditation: Closing the gates to the Satan. Forgetting all limited and limiting thoughts. Destroying negative influences at the seed level, thus preventing bad things from happening in the first place. Overcoming our reactive nature. Transforming chaos to miracles and wonders.

❸ תפארת, יום שלישי Tuesday, Tiferet   נגד יכש

נָ֣א גִבּ֔וֹר. דּוֹרְשֵׁ֥י יִחוּדְ֒ךָ. כְּבָבַ֖ת שָׁמְרֵֽם:

na   gibor   dorshei   yihudecha   kevavat   shomrem

Meditation: Connecting to all forms of sustenance, both physical and spiritual. Rejuvenating our body. Removing death from all aspects of life, including body, relationships, business. Gaining help to avoid speaking evil speech.

❹ נצח, יום רביעי Wednesday, Netzach   בטר צתג

בָּרְכֵ֣ם טַהֲרֵ֑ם. רַחֲמֵ֥י צִדְקָתְ֒ךָ. תָּמִ֖יד גָּמְלֵֽם:

barchem   taharem   rachamei   tzidkatecha   tamid   gomlem

Meditation: Persevering. Gaining the endurance to follow through and prove victorious in our spiritual work.

← Scanning Direction

Angel Intelligence

❺ הוד, יום חמישי Thursday, Hod   חקב טנע

חָסִין קָדוֹשׁ. בְּרוֹב טוּבְךָ. נַהֵל עֲדָתֶךָ:

chasin   kadosh   berov   tuvecha   nahel   adatecha

Meditation: Seeing the big picture, thus gaining deep insight and clairvoyance into how we can connect to the Light and bring the Light to ourselves and the world.

❻ יסוד, יום שישי Friday, Yesod   יגל פזק

יָחִיד גֵּאֶה. לְעַמְּךָ פְּנֵה. זוֹכְרֵי קְדוּשָּׁתֶךָ:

yachid   ge'eh   le'amecha   penei   zochrei   kedushatecha

Meditation: Feeling a desire to enlighten others. Bringing spirituality to the world by spreading the wisdom of Kabbalah. Finding peace and inner tranquility.

❼ מלכות, שבת Saturday, Malchut   שקו צית

שַׁוְעָתֵנוּ קַבֵּל. וּשְׁמַע צַעֲקָתֵנוּ. יוֹדֵעַ תַּעֲלוּמוֹת:

shav'atenu   kabel   ushma   tza'akatenu   yode'a   ta'alumot

Meditation: Gaining the power of renewal and restoration.

(בלחש) בָּרוּךְ שֵׁם כְּבוֹד מַלְכוּתוֹ, לְעוֹלָם וָעֶד:

(silently)   baruch   shem   kevod   malchuto   le'olam   va'ed

◄ Scanning Direction

Kabbalah Centre Books

72 Names of God, The: Technology for the Soul
72 Names of God for Kids, The: A Treasury of Timeless Wisdom
72 Names of God Meditation Book, The
And You Shall Choose Life: An Essay on Kabbalah, the Purpose of Life, and Our True Spiritual Work
AstrologiK: Kabbalistic Astrology Guide for Children
Becoming Like God: Kabbalah and Our Ultimate Destiny
Beloved of My Soul: Letters of Our Master and Teacher Rav Yehuda Tzvi Brandwein to His Beloved Student, Kabbalist Rav Berg
Consciousness and the Cosmos (Previously Star Connection)
Days of Connection: A Guide to Kabbalah's Holidays and New Moons
Days of Power Part 1
Days of Power Part 2
Education of a Kabbalist
Energy of the Hebrew Letters, The
Fear is Not an Option
Finding the Light Through the Darkness: Inspirational Lessons Rooted in the Bible and the Zohar
God Wears Lipstick: Kabbalah for Women
Holy Grail, The: A Manifesto on the Zohar
Immortality: The Inevitability of Eternal Life
Kabbalah Connection, The: Preparing the Soul for Pesach
Kabbalah for the Layman
Kabbalah Method, The: The Bridge Between Science and the Soul, Physics and Fulfillment, Quantum and the Creator
Kabbalah: The Power To Change Everything
Kabbalistic Astrology: And the Meaning of Our Lives
Kabbalistic Bible: Genesis
Kabbalistic Bible: Exodus
Kabbalistic Bible: Leviticus

Kabbalistic Bible: Numbers
Kabbalistic Bible: Deuteronomy
Light of Wisdom: On Wisdom, Life, and Eternity
Miracles, Mysteries, and Prayer Volume 1
Miracles, Mysteries, and Prayer Volume 2
Nano: Technology of Mind Over Matter
Navigating The Universe: A Roadmap for Understanding the Cosmic Influences that Shape Our Lives (Previously Time Zones)
On World Peace: Two Essays by the Holy Kabbalist Rav Yehuda Ashlag
Path to the Light: Decoding the Bible with Kabbalah: Book of Beresheet Volume 1
Path to the Light: Decoding the Bible with Kabbalah: Book of Beresheet Volume 2
Path to the Light: Decoding the Bible with Kabbalah: Book of Beresheet Volume 3
Path to the Light: Decoding the Bible with Kabbalah: Book of Beresheet Volume 4
Path to the Light: Decoding the Bible with Kabbalah: Book of Shemot Volume 5
Path to the Light: Decoding the Bible with Kabbalah: Book of Shemot Volume 6
Path to the Light: Decoding the Bible with Kabbalah: Book of Vayikra Volume 7
Path to the Light: Decoding the Bible with Kabbalah: Book of Bamdibar Volume 8
Path to the Light: Decoding the Bible with Kabbalah: Book of Bamdibar Volume 9
Power of Kabbalah, The: 13 Principles to Overcome Challenges and Achieve Fulfillment
Rethink Love: 3 Steps to Being the One, Attracting the One, and Becoming One
Satan: An Autobiography
Secret, The: Unlocking the Source of Joy & Fulfillment
Secrets of the Bible: Teachings from Kabbalistic Masters

Secrets of The Zohar: Stories and Meditations to Awaken the Heart
Simple Light: Wisdom from a Woman's Heart
Shabbat Connections
Taming Chaos: Harnessing the Secret Codes of the Universe to Make Sense of Our Lives
Thought of Creation, The: On the Individual, Humanity, and Their Ultimate Perfection
To Be Continued: Reincarnation & the Purpose of Our Lives
To the Power of One
True Prosperity: How to Have Everything
Two Unlikely People to Change the World: A Memoir by Karen Berg
Vokabbalahry: Words of Wisdom for Kids to Live By
Way of the Kabbalist, The: A User's Guide To Technology for the Soul
Well of Life: Kabbalistic Wisdom from a Depth of Knowledge
Wheels of the Soul: Kabbalah and Reincarnation
Wisdom of Truth, The: 12 Essays by the Holy Kabbalistn Rav Yehuda Ashlag
Zohar, The

BOOKS AVAILABLE AT
STORE.KABBALAH.COM
AND KABBALAH CENTRES AROUND THE WORLD

About the Centres

Below is a statement written by Rav Berg in 1984. It remains true today.

Through the ultimate knowledge and mystical practices of Kabbalah, one can reach the highest spiritual levels attainable. Although many people rely on belief, faith, and dogmas in pursuing the meaning of life, Kabbalists seek a spiritual connection with the Creator and the forces of the Creator, so that the strange becomes familiar, and faith becomes knowledge.

Throughout history, those who knew and practiced the Kabbalah were extremely careful in their dissemination of the knowledge because they knew the masses of mankind had not yet prepared for the ultimate truth of existence. Today, kabbalists know that it is not only proper but necessary to make the Kabbalah available to all who seek it.

The Kabbalah Centre is an independent, non-profit institute founded in Israel in 1922. The Centre provides research, information, and assistance to those who seek the insights of Kabbalah. The Centre offers public lectures, classes, seminars, and excursions to mystical sites at branches in Israel and in the United States. Branches have been opened in Mexico, Montreal, Toronto, Paris, Hong Kong, and Taiwan.

Our courses and materials deal with the Zoharic understanding of each weekly portion of the Torah. Every facet of life is covered and other dimensions, hithertofore unknown, provide a deeper connection to a superior reality. Three important beginner courses cover such aspects as: Time, Space and Motion; Reincarnation, Marriage, Divorce; Kabbalistic Meditation; Limitation of the Five Senses; Illusion-Reality; Four Phases; Male and Female, Death, Sleep, Dreams; Food; and Shabbat.

Thousands of people have benefited from the Centre's activities, and the Centre's publishing of kabbalistic material continues to be the most comprehensive of its kind in the world, including translations in English, Hebrew, Russian, German, Portuguese, French, Spanish, Farsi (Persian).

Kabbalah can provide one with the true meaning of their being and the knowledge necessary for their ultimate benefit. It can show one spirituality that is beyond belief. The Kabbalah Centre will continue to make available the Kabbalah to all those who seek it.

—Rav Berg, 1984

About The Zohar

The Zohar, the basic source of the Kabbalah, was authored two thousand years ago by Rabbi Shimon bar Yochai while hiding from the Romans in a cave in Peki'in for 13 years. It was later brought to light by Rabbi Moses de Leon in Spain, and further revealed through the Safed Kabbalists and the Lurianic system of Kabbalah.

The programs of The Kabbalah Centre have been established to provide opportunities for learning, teaching, research, and demonstration of specialized knowledge drawn from the ageless wisdom of the Zohar and the Jewish sages. Long kept from the masses, today this knowledge of the Zohar and Kabbalah should be shared by all who seek to understand the deeper meaning of this spiritual heritage, and a deeper and more profound meaning of life. Modern science is only beginning to discover what our sages veiled in symbolism. This knowledge is of a very practical nature and can be applied daily for the betterment of our lives and of humankind.

Darkness cannot prevail in the presence of Light. Even a darkened room must respond to the lighting of a candle. As we share this moment together we are beginning to witness, and indeed some of us are already participating in, a people's revolution of enlightenment. The darkened clouds of strife and conflict will make their presence felt only as long as the Eternal Light remains concealed.

The Zohar now remains an instrument to infuse the cosmos with the revealed Lightforce of the Creator. The Zohar is not a book about religion. Rather, the Zohar is concerned with the relationship between the unseen forces of the cosmos, the Lightforce, and the impact on humanity.

The Zohar promises that with the ushering in of the Age of Aquarius, the cosmos will become readily accessible to human understanding. It states that in the days of the Messiah "there will no longer be the necessity for one to request of his neighbor, teach me wisdom." (Zohar, Naso 9:65) "One day, they will no longer teach every man his neighbor and every man his brother, saying know the Lord. For they shall all know Me, from the youngest to the oldest of them. (Jeremiah 31:34) We can regain dominion of our lives and environment. To achieve this objective, the Zohar provides us with an opportunity to transcend the crushing weight of universal negativity.

The daily perusing of the Zohar, without any attempt at translation or understanding will fill our consciousness with the Light, improving our well-being, and influencing all in our environment toward positive attitudes. Even the scanning of the Zohar by those unfamiliar with the Hebrew Alef Bet will accomplish the same result.

The connection that we establish through scanning the Zohar is one of unity with the Light of the Creator. The letters, even if we do not consciously know Hebrew or Aramaic, are the channels through which the connection is made and can be likened to dialing a telephone number or typing in the codes to run a computer program. The connection is established at the metaphysical level of our being and radiates into our physical plane of existence. But first there is the prerequisite of metaphysical "fixing." We have to consciously, through positive thought and actions, permit the immense power of the Zohar to radiate love, harmony, and peace into our lives for us to share with all humanity and the universe.

As we enter the years ahead, the Zohar will continue to be a people's book, striking a sympathetic chord in the hearts and minds of those who long for peace, truth, and relief from suffering. In the face of crises and catastrophe, the Zohar has the ability to resolve agonizing human afflictions by restoring each individual's relationship with the Lightforce of the Creator.

— Rav Berg, 1984

Over four decades ago, Rav Berg and his wife Karen opened the doors of The Kabbalah Centre to all who desire to learn this universal wisdom. They set out to make the Light and wisdom of Kabbalah accessible and relevant to all people. Their goal was to teach the spiritual wisdom and provide the tools of Kabbalah, without exclusion. They believed that the study of Kabbalah would help people to live a better life, and that by doing so, the world would benefit. Under their leadership, The Kabbalah Centre has grown from a single location into one of the world's leading sources of spiritual wisdom, online and with more than 40 locations around the globe. Today The Kabbalah Centre provides instruction and community to tens of thousands of students.

Rav Berg made it his mission to continue editing, writing, printing, and distributing all that he learned from his teacher and began sharing the secrets of Kabbalah texts, which historically had been reserved for scholars. His book, Kabbalah for the Layman, was the revolutionary step that made Kabbalah accessible to every person. Rav Berg's other books include The Kabbalah Connection, Wheels of a Soul: Kabbalah and Reincarnation, To the Power of One, Energy of the Hebrew Letters, Immortality, Nano, The Kabbalah Method, Taming Chaos, and Education of a Kabbalist.

Following Rav Berg's passing in September 2013, Karen Berg untiringly lead and nurtured Kabbalah Centres around the world. As its Spiritual Director and Founder, Karen was devoted to an enduring vision, "within each person there is a spark of God that can be bound together to create transcendence beyond all differences."

Karen's books include God Wears Lipstick: Kabbalah for Women; Simple Light: Wisdom from a Woman's Heart; To Be Continued... Reincarnation and the Purpose of Our Lives; Finding the Light through the Darkness: Inspirational Lessons Rooted in the Bible and the Zohar; and Two Unlikely People to Change the World: A Memoir by Karen Berg.

Karen departed this world at the instant of sunrise on July 30th, 2020. According to the Hebrew calendar this was the 9th day of Av (Leo), considered one of the darkest days of the year, that paradoxically also possesses within it birth of enlightenment. Karen left the world just as she lived in it. "The darkest part of the night is just before the dawn," she would say, "this is meant to teach us that it is through the darkness that we find the Light." The Rav and Karen's lives are celebrated by four children, sixteen grandchildren, and a legacy of Light to the world.

Following their passing, their son Michael Berg continues their vision and their work as the Director of The Kabbalah Centre.

www.ingramcontent.com/pod-product-compliance
Lightning Source LLC
LaVergne TN
LVHW010307070426
835512LV00029B/3499